Sheffield
City Council

Renew this item at:
http://library.sheffield.gov.uk
or contact your local library

LIBRARIES, ARCHIVES & INFORMATION

FAMILY HISTORY FROM PEN & SWORD BOOKS

Birth, Marriage & Death Records
The Family History Web Directory
Tracing British Battalions on the Somme
Tracing Great War Ancestors
Tracing History Through Title Deeds
Tracing Secret Service Ancestors
Tracing the Rifle Volunteers
Tracing Your Air Force Ancestors
Tracing Your Ancestors
Tracing Your Ancestors from 1066 to 1837
Tracing Your Ancestors Through Death Records –
  Second Edition
Tracing Your Ancestors through Family Photographs
Tracing Your Ancestors Through Letters and
  Personal Writings
Tracing Your Ancestors Using DNA
Tracing Your Ancestors Using the Census
Tracing your Ancestors using the UK Timeline
Tracing Your Ancestors: Cambridgeshire, Essex,
  Norfolk and Suffolk
Tracing Your Aristocratic Ancestors
Tracing Your Army Ancestors
Tracing Your Army Ancestors – Third Edition
Tracing Your Birmingham Ancestors
Tracing Your Black Country Ancestors
Tracing Your Boer War Ancestors
Tracing Your British Indian Ancestors
Tracing Your Canal Ancestors
Tracing Your Channel Islands Ancestors
Tracing Your Church of England Ancestors
Tracing Your Criminal Ancestors
Tracing Your Docker Ancestors
Tracing Your East Anglian Ancestors
Tracing Your East End Ancestors
Tracing Your Family History on the Internet
Tracing Your Female Ancestors
Tracing Your First World War Ancestors
Tracing Your Freemason, Friendly Society and
  Trade Union Ancestors
Tracing Your Georgian Ancestors, 1714–1837
Tracing Your Glasgow Ancestors
Tracing Your Great War Ancestors: The Gallipoli
  Campaign

Tracing Your Great War Ancestors: The Somme
Tracing Your Great War Ancestors: Ypres
Tracing Your Huguenot Ancestors
Tracing Your Insolvent Ancestors
Tracing Your Irish Family History on the Internet
Tracing Your Jewish Ancestors
Tracing Your Jewish Ancestors – Second Edition
Tracing Your Labour Movement Ancestors
Tracing Your Legal Ancestors
Tracing Your Liverpool Ancestors
Tracing Your Liverpool Ancestors – Second
  Edition
Tracing Your London Ancestors
Tracing Your Medical Ancestors
Tracing Your Merchant Navy Ancestors
Tracing Your Northern Ancestors
Tracing Your Northern Irish Ancestors
Tracing Your Northern Irish Ancestors – Second
  Edition
Tracing Your Oxfordshire Ancestors
Tracing Your Pauper Ancestors
Tracing Your Police Ancestors
Tracing Your Potteries Ancestors
Tracing Your Pre-Victorian Ancestors
Tracing Your Prisoner of War Ancestors: The First
  World War
Tracing Your Railway Ancestors
Tracing Your Roman Catholic Ancestors
Tracing Your Royal Marine Ancestors
Tracing Your Rural Ancestors
Tracing Your Scottish Ancestors
Tracing Your Second World War Ancestors
Tracing Your Servant Ancestors
Tracing Your Service Women Ancestors
Tracing Your Shipbuilding Ancestors
Tracing Your Tank Ancestors
Tracing Your Textile Ancestors
Tracing Your Twentieth-Century Ancestors
Tracing Your Welsh Ancestors
Tracing Your West Country Ancestors
Tracing Your Yorkshire Ancestors
Writing Your Family History
Your Irish Ancestors

TRACING YOUR FAMILY HISTORY WITH THE WHOLE FAMILY

A Family Research Adventure for All Ages

ROBIN C. McCONNELL

Pen & Sword
FAMILY HISTORY

First published in Great Britain in 2022 by
PEN AND SWORD FAMILY HISTORY
An imprint of
Pen & Sword Books Ltd
Yorkshire – Philadelphia

ISBN 978 1 39901 388 8

Typeset by Mac Style
Printed and bound in the UK by CPI Group (UK) Ltd,
Croydon, CR0 4YY.

Pen & Sword Books Limited incorporates the imprints of Atlas,
Archaeology, Aviation, Discovery, Family History, Fiction, History,
Maritime, Military, Military Classics, Politics, Select, Transport,
True Crime, Air World, Frontline Publishing, Leo Cooper, Remember
When, Seaforth Publishing, The Praetorian Press, Wharncliffe
Local History, Wharncliffe Transport, Wharncliffe True Crime
and White Owl.

For a complete list of Pen & Sword titles please contact

PEN & SWORD BOOKS LIMITED
47 Church Street, Barnsley, South Yorkshire, S70 2AS, England
E-mail: enquiries@pen-and-sword.co.uk
Website: www.pen-and-sword.co.uk

Or

PEN AND SWORD BOOKS
1950 Lawrence Rd, Havertown, PA 19083, USA
E-mail: Uspen-and-sword@casematepublishers.com
Website: www.penandswordbooks.com

**This Book is Dedicated
To**

Diana Jayne Olsen (née McConnell)
Family Historian & Sister Extraordinaire.

And

*Penny Zipfel, Kit McConnell,
Maya Zipfel, Cleo Zipfel, Sophia McConnell,
Toby McConnell.*
Bearers of the learning of life history.

CONTENTS

ACKNOWLEDGEMENTS

This book had considerable assistance from family and friends. The author's sister, Jayne Olsen, has been instrumental in her role as the key family genealogist. Barbara Hay has been a family history leader in the Coates-Coleman field which led to exampled realities noted in the present text. Special thanks for assistance with proofreading go to my daughter, Penny Zipfel, and to Gaynor Haliday for her thorough, and especially professional, editing and proofreading.

My son, Kit McConnell, has fostered a strong sense of historical time and place which is reflected in various parts of the text. Maya and Cleo Zipfel have the author's warm regard for their suggestions and ability to recount family history that set the scene for real-life elements of inclusion. Compiling the Cornes/Waite family tree with Lorraine Beven provided tests of the text's practicality. Judi Brennan's grandchildren, Sophia and Harry Blewett, led to further considerations of what young children should learn about their family history lineage. Special thanks to Sophia and Toby McConnell for their theme photograph.

INTRODUCTION

This book is different from family history books that assume research will be carried out only by adults. It has twin goals of generating family history interests with all ages of present family members and providing practical guidelines for them on how researching family history can become an exciting whole-family enterprise. Thoughtful parents, and thoughtful genealogists working with families, can initiate a research adventure rather than an imposition leading to young family members exhibiting boredom, disinterest or even resistance. Each family member, as part of the family team, can be involved in researching their past family history and generate, for future generations, a picture of their present family history. When we know our family's history more completely, we then know ourselves more completely.

It is comparatively difficult for family leaders to locate satisfactory books providing practical advice on family members of all ages being involved in family history research. It is rare to find writing on family history with guidance for all members of a present-day family presenting their lives of today as part of the family's future. True researchers intuit that when you research for 'your self' you research for 'other selfs'.

The definition that has guided the author, in his research as an experienced genealogist, continues to be *'family history is a history of the direct family in the past and in the present – recorded for the future'*. It is this primary definition that underpins this book as it introduces family history and its research – past, present and future – as a team effort by all of the family, young and old. Using the definition as a basis will assure the family of success in researching its history.

This definition does not exclude researching other past members of the wider family, as such research can throw light upon the family and times of our direct line and can yield interesting collateral ancestors. However, for the family that has not researched its family's history or not drawn children and young family members into their research, the starting point and centrality of their initial research is the direct family line for, say, four or five past generations. This provides a more certain achievement of success, which can be built upon and later expanded to become research of the 'whole' past family.

This book explains how to involve all the family, regardless of prior experience, age, education, research experience or computer skills, in undertaking research of their family's history and recording their family's present setting for future descendants. It offers, for the experienced family historian parent, a range of considerations for expanding this usually adult activity by bringing the whole family into family history research. It provides, for the inexperienced family historian parent, a path towards their becoming a genealogist who will energise and lead all family members into this new phase of family life.

One emphasis is upon all your family moving forward into the past. The other emphasis is upon them moving forward from the present to the future as they assemble their research of the past, and full account of the family today, that may be handed down to the family of tomorrow. Certain sites are noted in the text to assist family leaders with these two emphases and Appendix I sets out supportive further resources. There are tens of thousands of possible genealogical sites, many of which disappear from the ether or will newly appear tomorrow. In this book, the critical use of search engines is frequently drawn upon, especially to locate specialised sources. There is a core set of research sites, in Appendix 1, provided as primary and free sites which are essential to explore, and return to at intervals in your family's research.

Your family can develop positively from the family history knowledge they will acquire, the stories of which they become part and the narrative journey to learn more about who they are. The author has noted the positive impact of family history becoming a shared journey that enhances identity and positive perceptions of self. No researcher of worth will feel they stand alone. There is objective university research that shows this and the value of family history familiarity in enhancing identity and emotional well-being. Knowing family history can foster your son or daughter's positive qualities. (See Fivush, Duke and Bohanek, 2010).

The concepts of family leadership and developing your family as a team for any major undertaking are rarely considered, but these underpin what can become a whole-family research adventure. Your family, at best, is not a disparate assemblage of individuals but developing as a team of individuals, with agreed goals, who cohere and strive for themselves, for each other and with each other. Practical understandings of the family team concept assist families to become more unified and assured in their joint project.

Family history research can develop greater family unity and seed a knowledge and motivation that may well be carried by younger family members into their futures. Later generations will enjoy pictures, diaries and records from children that illustrate their lives of today. Research (see bibliography) strongly supports the benefits of children (and elderly persons) being involved with family history as listeners and participants. Check for yourself the online availability of writing on 'benefits for children doing family history'.

The author's grandchildren have learned stories associated with family members, whether centuries old or recent. The terminal illness of one brother and unexpected death of another led to the remaining brother and sister writing a range of reminiscences from childhood and youthful years that are now part of their direct family history, confidently told by grandchildren to other family members and friends, especially tales of their grandfather and his siblings growing up.

And, did great-great-grandpa Kensington really make up 'his song' that he always sang or recited, 'Sitting in the Kennel with the Bulldog Pup?' Children and grandchildren are keen to hear stories of their parents and earlier generations when they were young. It may be that this link of stories and real ancestors is how children develop genuine interests in their family's history. There is always a passage into the past that will intrigue our children of the present. Different ancestral branches of the author's families have migrated to New Zealand, USA, Canada and Australia. Today, cousins live in four countries. The finding of the emigration ship diaries and historical newspaper reports give today's youngsters their first understanding of the challenges of shipboard travel in the 1800s. Photographs and memorabilia are often the gates that open pathways for today's youngsters. Becoming aware of a family tree stimulates curiosity. 'Who is this person?'

Cleo, the 9-year-old piano player, asked if anyone in the family had played the piano before her. She was told of Courtney Kenny, the gifted pianist in England who shares her Kenny ancestry. I explained that when my mother died, her closest lifetime friend wrote an account of their friendship, stating that when my mother left high school, she had to decide whether to be a nurse or a concert pianist. Regrettably, her children and grandchildren had not known that while she was alive – a poignant indicator to all family historians to interview their parents and grandparents or receive memoirs from them.

The family home had no piano and one would have been bought for our mother if we had known of this strong element in her younger life. That is the power of knowing, or not knowing, our family members and their individual realities. We simply did not know our mother's history well enough.

The formation of a family history timeline, a historical event timeline and the construction of simple family tree outlines become excellent reference materials for young and old. These were recalled when Maya, then 11 years of age, telephoned to say she had a major school assignment to do on any chosen Christmas topic. 'Didn't one of our family have something special to do with Handel, the composer of the *Messiah*?' The first public performance of *Messiah* on 13 April 1742 came

The pianist or nurse career choice for Norma Bessie Kensington (1916–1979).

through the permission of the Church of England Deans of Christ Church and St Patrick's cathedrals in Dublin for the oratorio to use their choirs for the public presentation which would raise money for three charities: prisoners' relief, the Mercer's Hospital, and the Charitable Infirmary. The deans of the two cathedrals were Gabriel James Maturin, the central figure in inviting Handel, and Jonathan Swift. Handel arrived in Dublin in November 1741, gathered an orchestra, had his chorus drawn from the city's two cathedrals, and worked with them to present *Messiah*. Clearly, Maya enjoyed knowing her direct Maturin ancestor knew Handel, and Swift, the author of Gulliver's Travels.

These examples illustrate the enjoyment of family history when key elements are known by the family. With parental and grandparent support, your youngsters will increasingly show initiative and develop considerable internet research skills to find more information. The bonding this brings is to be valued in any family.

A strong conclusion, from generating youngsters' interests in their forebears, is that family history can foster a sense of an investigative challenge in each family member. Parents and grandparents can stimulate the concept of making family history a research adventure. An adventure has overtones of enterprise, excitement and discovery. The stimulation of genealogical exploration and discoveries can readily lead young family members to unexpected feelings of success, joy and learning. Rather than being 'something that mum and dad do', family history then becomes 'something that we do'.

Primary Sites and Free Sites

While involving the whole family in family history research may foster family development and well-being, it can be demanding. It generates findings that bridge past, present and future and the overwhelming number of family history sites and sources online and in print present the challenge: which sites and resources do we select? To get an understanding of the breadth of genealogy sites online, browse the Wikipedia 'List of Genealogy Databases'. Given the plethora of genealogical sites, there is an emphasis in this book upon readily using search engines and noting their results, to work from and beyond. Search engines are listed in Chapter 2. Key genealogy sites are noted in the text and listed in Appendix 1.

Chapter 1 examines the meaning of family history and explores what may be viewed as a new and sustaining definition for developing full family involvement. It guides family heads into adopting a vision of family leadership that is challenging, rewarding and enhances family unity. Basic genealogical research and major research sites are discussed in this chapter to assist parents who want them at hand or may be inexperienced in family history research. Developing your basic knowledge of such family history sites and research methods, thorough careful planning prior to launching the innovative family venture, is essential.

Chapter 2 contributes critical preparations for a family gathering to launch the new family research venture. This initial time together requires thoughtful and knowledgeable planning. Building this preparation into actuality is Chapter 3, discussing that first family history 'togethering'. The goal of this critical time together is to 'sell' the idea, its challenges, its pleasures and benefits for present and future family members. The chapter addresses essential considerations of getting all family members involved, particularly children. The realisation builds that something stimulating for everyone arises from centring upon our definition of family history.

Moving into family research, the starting point is to get information from the eldest family members, usually grandparents or relatives of the grandparents' generation. Chapter 4 provides full guidance for younger family members interviewing their grandparents and relatives to elicit understandings of their lives and to personally gain family history information.

The major domain of early research that readily allows researchers to make no-cost errors is that of moving into free online family history sites. In Chapter 5 these are featured, along with activities and sources more expansive than simply noting such online sites. As with all chapters, there is the continuing theme of practicalities in helping the full range of family members participate in what are, almost definitely, new roles.

Children can become remarkable historians. Chapter 6 relates to preceding chapters but moves beyond them to provide practical guidance in stimulating children's roles and contributions to the family's research. Children of all ages are considered through this book with practical ideas provided. Research shows that 'pre-adolescent children who know more about their family history display higher levels of emotional well-being' (p.1, Fivush, Duke and Bohanek, 2010). Methods and activities, sometimes noted in one chapter as suitable for a particular age group, are flexible and transferable, depending upon youngsters' interests, attitudes and online search abilities.

Teenagers have Chapter 7, which addresses their involvement in exciting challenges of family research. It provides activities which they can undertake, yielding results that enhance knowledge of the family's direct past. They will contribute to the future family's knowledge of the teenagers' present-day family and gain personally in their emotional well-being, redistribution of experience and a more confident sense of self.

There is often a marked potential for linkages between home and school with elements of family history being considered in school curricula activities. Chapter 8 discusses opportunities for these and offers suggestions that can enhance the home-school relationship through family history research and classroom subjects.

Chapter 9 provides the family with suggestions that assist members to creatively record their past and present family history. These range from pre-school children's activities to the contributions that can come from parents, grandparents and members of the wider family.

The final chapter, Chapter 10, looks ahead in your family history venture. The family, in its real achievements in researching family history, individually and collectively, faces the question of what best to do with the results. We are researching the past and the present for the future. How then, do we best pass on our findings to descendants of today's family? Ways that today's family members can pass on their family history research results, and insightful presentations of their present family life, are outlined. The family reunion is an excellent step for the wider family to take in moving forward and is included in the practical orientation of this chapter.

Listed sites for sourcing genealogical data, and a realistic case study of a 'whole family in action' researching their family history, are the bases of the two appendices in this book.

Chapter 1

A NEW PERSPECTIVE ON FAMILY HISTORY?

Family history is a history of the direct family in the past and in the present – recorded for the future.

This is a new perspective for many family history researchers. 'Direct family', in the present definition, is used to emphasise that we are undertaking our research, with our home family of various ages, anchored to the focus of a direct family line. We research our predecessors for our knowledge today and pass that knowledge to our family of tomorrow. Implicit in our definition is the recording of our present-day family life, for our descendants.

The conventional emphasis of genealogical research is that family history is a history of the family in the past, recorded today. Usually implicit in this attitude is that the research is undertaken by adults. However, consciously seeking the direct family line has five important aspects for the young researchers in your family.

1. It will reward today's researching family with an enhanced knowledge and understanding of their family's past. We are, because they were.
2. It underscores the concept that all people are of worth and each of our earlier family members has contributed to our present being.
3. The concept of researching the direct family stimulates the growth of individual research skills and our ability to think laterally, with inherent challenges for each of the family researchers. This often leads to valued discussions between younger and older present-day family members on problem-solving research methods. It leads to new learning and an enhanced knowledge of history, especially social history.

4. Seeking knowledge of their family can be a positive force in drawing a present-day family together. There is enjoyment, sharing pursuits that generate self-confidence and numerous opportunities for warm family interaction.

5. With the centrality of our research being the direct family line for, say, five generations, we do not have an endless goal and are virtually assured of results that inform, and enervate, our present-day family.

Our present is the future's past: *family history is a history of the direct family in the past and in the present – recorded for the future.* This is a ready stimulus to bring all our family into the family history as it is inclusive of the family's present-day lives and achievements. Our genealogy comes alive with personal relevance for each family member when they recognise that family history happened in the past, is happening in the present and provides a record for the future. The family will come to realise that sound family history, like sound family ethics, will honour the past, value the present and safeguard the future. Safeguarding the future knowledge of our descendants is critical as we need to pass on accurate and informative records.

Collateral Ancestors and Collateral Descendants

In starting your family research, it is helpful to focus, initially perhaps, on five generations, starting with your children. These generations are relatively straightforward and have abundant records once we know where to look. The five-generation search immediately brings our children into the direct family line as they are the base of this initial portrayal of immediate past generations. Clearly, this enhances emotional and enquiry responses which underpin identity and foster young ones' desire to 'find out'. Later, we can draw upon our gathered findings and move to research the family, rather than only our direct line of the family.

Although our usual focus is upon the direct ancestral line, we often find, when blocked on that direct line, that we can explore wider family lines through close relatives of our direct ancestors and these lines often add to our direct family line knowledge. We have collateral relatives in two domains: collateral ancestors, the relatives who are not of our direct ancestral line but were linked closely to that line and collateral descendants, who will be closely linked with our direct descendants, being siblings or cousins, for example, of those descendants.

A clear example of collateral ancestral pursuit came through researching our direct line of Bernard (Bryan) Coleman and Anne Coleman (née Morgan) of Dundalk, when we discovered a daughter, Isabella (Bella)

Maglin Coleman (1860–1934), who was a sister of the author's great-grandmother. Bella, our collateral ancestor, was a missionary in China from 1891 to 1927 (including furloughs) and experienced the Boxer Rebellion. She lived an extraordinary life of commitment to her beliefs. She learned Chinese, dressed in Chinese clothing and served at a mission station 1,000 miles (1,609km) from the sea. She strongly criticised European nations taking over areas of China.

'Aunt Bella's' affectionate letters to her siblings from China in the 1890s illustrate research beyond the direct family line when third cousins of the author were found, in 2020, who had some of her original letters. The whole family vista came through her descriptions of living history and her knowledge of lives being lived by her siblings' children at homes far distant from China. Her collateral ancestor letters often mentioned our direct line ancestors with information we would not have otherwise known. It is difficult to imagine any child or family member not responding to the timeline Bella was in, the excitement of her letters, the mentions of direct ancestors and learning of a way of life markedly different from theirs.

Memorabilia: The mother-of-pearl piece from a family missionary in China.

An example of a collateral descendant, of a great-grandfather, was my mother's cousin who had no children but gave valued direct line family inheritance to her cousin's son.

Every family has the potential for unearthing their Isabella equivalent – perhaps one of the family who left letters which inform of a direct ancestor, who lived an unexpected life or who is found through a newspaper, DNA results or Google search. These rewarding and often enriching dimensions of our family research add to knowledge of our direct line, which is the continuing focal point of our present research.

Considerations of Young Family Members

Concomitant with family members' research and presenting accounts of their present lives for future generations, will come enhanced relationships, more relevant understandings of the past and each family participant feeling valued. Initially, young family members may not see the relevance of their present-day lives as important dimensions of their family history. However, parents' questions evoke a personal interest in family history from young children. 'Would you like to read about Nana and her pets when she was 7 years old?' or 'Grandad kept a diary of staying with his aunt and uncle on their farm seventy years ago. Would you like to read it?' 'An old friend of your great-grandfather works in an air museum where they have a plane the same as he used to fly. He would like to show it to you and said you could sit in the pilot's seat, which they don't usually let visitors do.' 'Did you know anything special about Grandma and the county fair?' 'I wonder why this girl in the mini-skirt looks like you, Aunt Sarah-Jane.'

There is an enjoyable challenge for family leaders to plan thoroughly for a stimulating first family gathering to launch the all-in family history research venture. Parents and older family siblings can help youngsters see how present-day lives can become valuable segments of their contemporary history when set out for future descendants – the yet-to-come generations of the family. When explained with clarity and enthusiasm, then supported sensitively and knowledgeably, all family members will find a stimulating and progressive engagement with their family history.

Children of any age can illustrate their weekly lives, special days and records for the future in varied ways. This leads to present-day family decisions on what to pass on to future descendants and how this will be done. Future generations will benefit from the insights they gain on your lives of today – the family in the present, recorded for the family in the future.

The recording of your present family life, with all its multiplicity, opens exciting possibilities for children. From the youngest to the elderly, all have present-day contributions to provide for future generations. The baby has fingerprints, is the subject of photographs and can be caught on video, often in interaction with an older sibling. The young ones can draw, paint, write, keep a fortnight's diary and be interviewed about their home life. The motivated 9-year-old can help her younger brother understand his immediate past family. The engaging writing of our selves is writing for 'our selves' and for 'other selves'. The present-day family has opportunities to encourage young family members in their research use of online sites. Underpinning the overall project should be a balance of the young ones' exploratory research with appropriate support and guidance from others in the family.

Researching the past of your family usually starts with knowledge gained from parents, grandparents, extended family, close friends and previous researchers. The initial searches are to locate birth, marriage and death dates, electoral rolls, census data and finding past newspaper references to direct line ancestors. Then searchers invariably move on to researching more specific sites, names, locations and more diverse genealogical resources triggered by their initial forays. Research skills become transferable and are quickly applied to the free sites. Then today's researcher, young or old, experienced or inexperienced, usually moves to search international compilations of information held by major organisations such as Findmypast, Ancestry, FamilySearch, MyHeritage and TheGenealogist. With enhanced self-confidence, our young family members quickly become adept at utilising social media such as Facebook, Twitter and YouTube to locate their genealogical streams and will want to have family DNA tests.

The recording of research adventure results will need planning and later bring a range of possibilities, from the standard written record of the present family to possibilities rendered by the imagination, such as time capsules, artworks, personal life histories, photographs, creative writing, video productions, social media, storing files and family trees in Cloud sharing, a family blog or newsletter and lodging information on international sites.

Relationships are enhanced through a mutual research adventure, particularly across generations and within the wider family. Tracing your ancestors is a research process that generates interaction, assistance, learning across age groups, sibling interaction and parent-child interaction. It can generate higher levels of mutual understanding, especially as parents, at times, will be learning from their children.

A serious goal is that of bringing all family members into the project and, increasingly, handing the family history to them. Today's young family members will be the next generation bearers of your family's history. What would you wish them to take into their future? What should they provide to future family members? Can the young ones add to the knowledge of their parents? A teenager who contacted a diverse group of his parents' childhood friends revived friendships for them and their memories contributed insightful, and sometimes humorous stories, about the researched family. They also reflected to the teen how some elements in a parent are the elements in them.

You may have adopted children. Do carefully consider the interpersonal and legal dimensions of assisting them to pursue their birth families' lines, if this is appropriate, and if you have confidence in their ability and maturity to handle possible implications of the proposed research project. This family research adventure can markedly affirm their sense of self-worth and security of knowing their own birth family's history, especially with the knowledge that they are secure and supported in their adoptive family.

If you are a separated parent then, if circumstances permit, discuss with your ex-partner, or ex-spouse, the project you are planning. Keep them in touch with how it is progressing, as you move into the family history venture, and encourage their discussions with the children. The research could still focus upon both parental lines for your children and include, if appropriate, both sets of grandparents. Results can readily be shared, again, if circumstances permit. Ideally, both parents are involved in being informative and supportive.

With these caveats in mind, we turn to the first step in this innovative family project – thoughtful parents planning for initiating their family's involvement in the new and exciting venture.

Chapter 2

PREPARING FOR WHOLE FAMILY INVOLVEMENT

The most critical stage in developing your present family's involvement in family history research is this first stage. The new approach, of involving all your family members in the family history project, has the critical focus upon knowing your family, being confident with basic research and the possession of an adventurous spirit. With a clear conception of these, we prepare for, perhaps, a whole morning gathering of the family for the introduction and initiation of this remarkable family venture.

Assuming the family has parents or caregivers with responsibility for younger family members, we face a range of reflective considerations. Can we really do this together? Will each of us be involved? What is a family? Are we a group or are we a team?

Seriously consider how your young ones perceive the family and their roles in it. Some families may exist with no real sense of unity, common family goals or open communication. Consider family discussions that lead to genuine considerations of individual needs, heartfelt values and the personal sense of belonging. If you have a unified family, with buy-in from each family member, your family will be transformed in significant ways by researching its family history. There will be new feelings of belonging to a vitalised team, recognition of individual ideas and a family appreciation of sound research and creative solution finding.

The Family Team and Family Leadership

Instead of what is, too often, a family group, do consider your family as a team. Most of us have been involved with a team – in the workplace, in sport, community organisations, church etc. Underpinning any family team is a shared perception of family, of what it means to be in a supportive and energising family. As a team you have common beliefs about your purposes, you have a broad agreement on goals and an understanding of how these goals will be achieved. A family team has members who understand their roles. Teams have leaders who are agents of change. Family leaders see their team setting as a learning place.

A family team has parents as leaders and does not have the parents, primarily, as managers. A parent as family leader is different from the parent as family manager. Of course, there are managerial requirements of the former but the family leader deals with what shapes the family, whereas the family manager deals with what happens in the family; the leader is primarily proactive where the manager is reactive; the leader is committed to the family team's potential and imagination, whereas the manager is orientated to roles and organisational positions. The leader is orientated towards the emotional, uplifting, aspirational and relational, whereas the manager is more concerned with resources and family infrastructures. Consider these roles critically, in terms of developing your whole family's involvement in this family team research venture.

Leadership, in the context of this book, is an influence relationship, in a family context, through which the leader(s) and family members share a common vision and pursue agreed goals to which they are jointly and individually committed. (After McConnell, 2007; McConnell, 2011). At times, the leader of the family may be one of the younger members leading in a particular venture, piece of research or family development such as the family reunion. What do you consider as the realistic implications and actions of yourself as the family leader? How will others in your family, when appropriate, provide leadership to the family? How will you facilitate young ones acquiring leadership skills? Your leadership will make or break the family's research venture.

A family can operate in a transactional mode or a transformative mode. The former is a quid pro quo group where one member undertakes an action or responsibility for the receipt of pocket money or some sort of concession. There is no sense of family vision or mission underpinning this. The transformative family is more likely to unite and find challenge and excitement in bringing new results to the family. It has family team members being genuinely uplifted by the stimulating research in which they engage and share. Researching the family history then becomes an uplifting intellectual and emotional adventure. This has connotations of challenge, of excitement and risk. It implies, in the adventure sense, the opportunity for initiative and individual effort. In a real sense you are going to have the task of developing attitudes with youngsters that finding out about your family can be stimulating, pleasurable, challenging and achievable.

Family Membership

One family prepared for its first research gathering with questions for individuals, 'What does it mean to be in this family? What does it mean to be part of this family?' A noted arts therapist, based in one school to assist children, teachers and parents, asked a challenging pupil to provide a picture of what she felt as a family member. The student brought the drawing to the therapist. It showed the other family members in a group but the pupil herself was off to one side and not included in the family group.

This pupil's understanding teacher, after discussion with the therapist, decided to have a class assignment on 'Fifty Years of Your Family's History'. Methods of undertaking this were discussed in class and parents received a helpful note from the teacher. The child who had felt excluded from her family understood the questions to ask, some sites that might help when searched and how to obtain information from family members.

She consequently received one-to-one parental attention, older sibling assistance and engaging interviews with her grandparents. These led to completion of the assignment and, better yet, closer communication and enhanced understandings between the child and her parents and grandparents.

Making Research a Family Adventure

A 12-year-old family member stressed to the author that family research would become an adventure for youngsters 'If it is fun and entertaining and makes them [youngsters in the family] want to find out more. Give or show them some interesting information, something they would think is cool because that would make them want to learn more and see that there are more cool and interesting people or connections in their family.' Think of Maya's advice, your ancestors and what, or who, could be 'cool and interesting'.

There is excitement for youngsters embarking on a new usage of computer, social media and research skills. How can you use this forthcoming family research adventure for youngsters to learn more about seeking, organising and evaluating the validity of information? Will they understand implications of the information for further research?

Prepare a positive environment for implementing the family's research adventure. The whole-family engagement should make research relevant, enjoyable and challenging at an achievable level. It is a learning experience and results in the enhanced attainment of skills. Let's be guided by my daughter, when I forgot she was an intelligent teenager, who declared, 'Dad, don't talk down to me … '

There are challenges at each level of your family's skills and interests. Assemble resources for the research adventure and plan how they will appeal to each youngster. How will the family project be explained as an adventure without an over-use of that word? Make this intra-family project fun, informative and unique. What activities could really appeal to our children? What are your aims for younger family members in this project?

Gathering Knowledge Before the First Meeting

Determine your use of search engines. You will build upon your basic acquisition of genealogical knowledge by fully using search engines. Use search terms of 'family history' and 'genealogy' interchangeably. Find how to frame your search questions with specificity rather than generality. Check meta search engines such as Dogpile and Mamma. Then try a range of search engines. Feed the same research question into each search engine to get an idea of the information they provide. Try the following list:

- AOL
- Ask.com
- Baidu
- Bing
- DuckDuckGo
- Ecosia
- Google Earth
- Internet Archive
- Naver
- Yahoo
- Yandex

Explore the range of different search engines, e.g. Google Maps, Google Earth. Google Books, Google News Archive, Google Scholar and Google Translate.

Having gained an understanding of different search engines, and their potential use, the researcher can then utilise the preferred ones answering the following questions:

- How do I best involve children in family history research?
- How do I find a specific source [list, electoral roll, census, passenger list etc.]?
- How do I trace my family history?

- How do I utilise historical newspaper sites?
- What are the best free family history research sites?
- Where do I obtain [birth, marriage, death] lists [for a certain country]?
- Which [software] commercial resource is best for constructing my family tree online?
- Which family history [or genealogical] sites are top-rated?
- Which family history sites are best for finding compiled family trees?
- Which genealogy subscription sites are best value?
- Which is the best [country specific] family history research site?
- Which sites are most helpful to a novice genealogist?

Check search engine responses to the above questions. Check national and international family history sites for articles and information on starting family history research. Look at YouTube presentations and check possible podcasts and webinars on beginning family history research. Sites in Appendix 1 offer links to wide ranges of further sites.

Check the major family history sites in Appendix 1 and the free online sites. Consider how much you know, and might need to know, about online sources. Your constant is the massive free site of FamilySearch. You need an operational familiarity with Ancestry, Findmypast, MyHeritage and, perhaps, TheGenealogist. Do not rush your preparation. You might begin noting their access, information provision and ease of searching. Ask advice from genealogist friends.

You will be carefully considering which potential searches will best fit potential researchers in your family. Purchase copies of the magazines *Who Do You Think You Are? Family Tree Magazine* and *Family Tree* to compare their emphases, helpfulness of articles and strengths. Locate similar magazines and journals. Check their e-subscriptions and get on their free mailing lists. Locate helpful books or sites on engaging children with family history. Check a selection of these in Appendix 1.

Your library may have informative books and records such as electoral rolls, phone books, trade directories, unpublished local histories, DVDs on genealogy and histories of geographic areas linked with your family. Fiction books could be found, set in the time of an ancestor. Many libraries have free access to Ancestry. Do they allow 'children' to access Ancestry? Some libraries have books on genealogical research and operate an inter-loan system for borrowing specific books from other libraries.

Ask at your library, the Citizens Advice Bureau or its local equivalent about local genealogical groups. Check meetings in neighbourhood newspapers or library notice boards. Find family historians through word-of-mouth, at social occasions, at work or by checking with family and friends.

Taking Stock on Initial Preparation

Parents relatively new to family history will need to familiarise themselves with research sources with which their family members will soon engage. Doing this, without becoming immersed in detail, gives parents an excellent understanding of the research knowledge and information they will take to the first family session. It may help to read through Appendix 2 to see broadly how one family moved through the stages of researching their family history.

Preparing for family discussions of this shared research adventure is vital. What are your goals? What, then, are your objectives? How will these be attained? Perhaps they are to stimulate interest in the family tree and to draw each family member into a research adventure that will be worth their engagement. Perhaps you have briefed one interested youngster to show a younger one where they are on the family (five generations) tree. 'Now, Toby, can you show me mum and dad on here?'

Sophia helps Toby understand the basic starting point from him to his parents and grandparents.

What do you anticipate will become individual family members' goals? Break large goals into sets of smaller, attainable objectives. This is especially important to avoid youngsters being overwhelmed, struggling, lacking understanding or becoming disheartened.

Before your family's possible half-day focus on the proposed research adventure, you will have moved into the following achievements:

1. Made a clear list of things to do before the first family meeting.
2. Retrieved basic details of births, marriages and deaths of parents, grandparents and, possibly, great-grandparents.
3. Recorded additional family information through free sites.
4. Became familiar with primary research sites of Ancestry, Findmypast, FamilySearch and MyHeritage.
5. Following your new familiarity with the subscription sites you critically considered, decided which, if any, you will pay to join. Considered also if grandparents or others will be asked to help with these costs.
6. Compiled draft family trees for each parent and basic five-generation family and historical timelines.
7. Explored further sites based upon information gained from earlier searches, such as cemetery records, census returns and electoral rolls.
8. Developed a basic familiarity with sites for selected historical newspapers and made notes on interesting discoveries.
9. Perhaps checked upon National Archives, National Libraries, and specialist lists, such as immigration and passenger lists.
10. Planned for the organisation and storage of your own record results.
11. Made a tentative list of what will be done at the family get-together.
12. Made initial decisions on which aspect of research will appeal to which family member.
13. Understood, and accepted, the requirements for effective family team leadership.
14. Prepared for a positive environment in implementing the family's research adventure.
15. Planned for evaluation of the family meeting and your launching of the new venture.

The whole-family engagement should make research relevant, enjoyable and challenging at achievable levels. It will be a learning experience and result in the increased attainment of skills. It will generate assistance in fostering children's interests in their family history. If uncertain, utilise search engines to locate sites and information on the particular family member's interests and apply historical searches.

Make enhanced family trees. Compile a limited list of basal sites, new genealogical words for children to understand, research skills they may need, and contact details for wider family members.

MARRIAGE.

HAMILTON—KENSINGTON. On October ... at the residence of the bride's mother, Ormu, Tauranga, by the Rev. C. Jordan, B.A., Edward, fourth son of the Rev. T. Hamilton, B.A., late rector of Killorglin, Co Kerry, to Reutra Eleanor, fourth daughter of Charles Jephson Kensington Esq., late of Werton, Wilts, England.

MOTOR-CAR ACCIDENTS.

LADY KILLED AT WELLINGTON.

December 17th 1906

HER DAUGHTER SERIOUSLY INJURED.

MRS. KENSINGTON, wife of Mr. W. C. Kensington, Secretary for Lands, was killed on Monday evening by being run over by a motor-car at the foot of Bower-street, Wellington.

Mrs. Kensington, accompanied by her two daughters, the Misses Louisa and Olive Kensington, had been into the city during the afternoon, and the three were walking homewards along Lambton Quay shortly before five o'clock. When they reached Bower-street crossing, a fire brigade motor car, driven by a man named Spry, approached the same spot, bound for the Botanical Gardens, where a fire had broken out.

The car passed right over Mrs. Kensington's head, and she was killed instantaneously.

Miss Louisa Kensington was also thrown down, and was picked up, with a compound fracture of the left leg. Miss Olive Kensington was uninjured.

It is said that the motorman sounded his alarm, and swerved to avoid the ladies, but they became confused at the approach of the machine. Spry was previously engaged driving motors between Napier and Taupo.

MOTOR-CAR ACCIDENTS.

THE WELLINGTON FATALITY.

1406

VERDICT OF THE JURY.

THE CORONER DISAGREES.

An inquest was opened in Wellington on the 18th of December, concerning the death of Mrs. Kensington (wife of the Under-Secretary for Lands), who was killed by the fire brigade motor-car on the previous day. The evidence showed that death was instantaneous, and was due to accident. Deceased's head was crushed, but there were absolutely no abrasions of the body. The inquest was adjourned.

Wm. Chas. Kensington, husband of deceased said deceased was 55 years of age. He had seen from the window of his own office, in Government Buildings, that an accident had happened. Someone rushed up and told him that he was wanted. Instantly he went over and saw first his daughter and then his wife lying on the ground. As he was coming up an officer said to him that it was a wonder 20 people had not been run over considering the rate at which the motor swung round that corner.

The inquiry was continued on Thursday. The greater part of the evidence was with regard to the pace at which the car travelled along Lambton Quay, and turned into Bowen-street, on the day of the accident. The driver, Spry, took the car over the ground, and afterwards said he had gone about the same rate as on Monday. This was denied by some of the witnesses, who said the pace on Monday had been greater. Some of them contended that the car travelled at between 15 and 20 miles an hour, and had turned the corner at an unsafe speed. It seemed to be established that Mrs. Kensington and her daughters did not see the motor until it was practically on top of them.

The inquest was concluded on Friday. The Coroner, in summing up, said that on the occasion of the accident the ladies had not the slightest intimation that anything would cross their path. To him it appeared that in such a case, when a vehicle came suddenly round a corner and did damage, there was something blameworthy in the action of the person driving the car. The question was whether the car turned the corner with proper precautions to prevent injury. So far as he could make out, when the ladies first saw the car coming it could not have been more than 24ft from them. If so, they had just four seconds to get out of the way. Ought not the driver, instead of risking the chance of the ladies going fast or slow across the road, to have stopped dead until they were safely across? It seemed to him that it was great rashness to turn the corner at 12 or 15 miles an hour.

The jury, after an hour's deliberation, returned the following verdict:— "We are unanimously of opinion that Mrs. Kensington met her death by accident and misadventure, by being knocked down by a motor fire engine, and that no blame is attachable to the driver of the engine, as we are convinced from the evidence that he saw a clear course when turning into Bowen-street. We are of opinion that the fire engine warnings are not distinct enough from the electric tram warning bell; that something that should be recognised as a fire engine alarm should be procured; and that stringent regulations should be brought into force regulating the speed of all motor vehicles." The jury tendered their sincere sympathy with the bereaved family.

The Coroner said he was bound to accept the verdict, but he wished to say he disagreed with it, particularly in view of the evidence tendered regarding the rate of speed at which the engine rounded the Bowen-street corner.

The death of Amy Kensington in local newspapers.

Optional Extended Pre-Gathering Research

With your family knowledge, you might wish to roam through sources, even from another country, that further broaden your knowledge and enhance your confidence. This is not essential before the family gathering but may include some, or all, of the following:

- Archives, national and local
- Blogs
- Books, such as local histories
- Cemetery records
- Census returns
- Certificates of births, deaths and marriages
- Chart suppliers
- Church and religion records
- Diaries and journals retained in a branch of the family
- District newspapers
- Electoral rolls
- Facebook and social media genealogy strains
- Family friends to be interviewed
- FamilySearch Local Facilities (Family History centres, Heritage centres)
- Genealogical publishers
- Genealogy and family history societies
- Home and land ownership records
- Legal papers, e.g. name changes, divorce and separation records
- Libraries
- Local History societies
- Magazines for family historians
- Materials that may be held by members of the wider family
- Medical records
- Meetings of local history, family history and interest groups
- Military records
- Museums
- National genealogical sources
- Newspapers
- Non-governmental archives
- Podcasts
- School histories, commemorative booklets and basic school records
- Sources in the recommended books
- Telephone books
- Town and regional organisations, e.g. trade unions, community service
- Trade and professional directories
- Wills

Such discoveries all help build up more information on your family's two timelines: your family member timeline with key dates and happenings; and a historical events timeline of dates and happenings in history. The family member dates can lead to seeking contemporary events and the historical dates can stimulate enquiry into ancestors' links with them.

Are there any past family notebooks, journals or diaries that you can access? These may be 'in the family somewhere', in archives or with local history societies. Check with collateral relatives. Not only do these records give you settings and happenings of earlier family members but, for the discerning researcher, there will be discoveries of people and places that are worth following up and tracing. In the author's family, his great-grandfather's 1890s surveyor's notebook had wonderful handwritten pages of their Kensington and De la Porte ancestry, going back some hundreds of years in Wiltshire and London for Kensingtons and through Huguenot lines to France for the De la Porte and Plumail families. Written from memory, the records correlated substantially with a range of subsequent research searches but did contain some seeming inaccuracies. Admittedly, that was a rarely found treasure.

The grocer's notebook of a grandfather in a different ancestral line had, amongst the intriguing grocery records and staff payments of his early twentieth-century grocery shop, addresses of relatives that ultimately led family researchers, some ninety years later, to learning of this grandfather's previously unknown sister, her married name and location in Scotland. In the notebook, family researchers located the invaluable handwritten entry of 'William McConnell Born 10 August 1845 and sailed from Portrush, Ireland, first time, 15 May 1860, for Glasgow, Scotland'. There was also the McConnell family Bible, passed down through generations, with its written records of ancestors' births, marriages and deaths, to hand on to future generations.

It is strongly advised that you obtain blank family ancestry charts at a range of levels of detail. Obtain pie charts, three-generation, four-generation or five-generation family tree sheets and a couple of nine- or twelve-generation charts. You could give out copies of these aids to each of the family at your first family gathering. Magazines such as *Family Tree Magazine* and other sites offer free charts.

Ensure you will guide the family in how to obtain information, record information and be able to follow possible leads from it. Inform them of free sites. Have multiple photocopies of recording pages ready for use by family members from the time of their initial family meeting. The spare copies allow for errors of entry in first uses of these. Does any family member know how to make spreadsheets?

Explain the use of searching newspaper sources. These cover millions of pages across various countries and some go back to the eighteenth century. Whichever you choose, for example Newspaper Archives in Great Britain, there may well be a direct family individual whose name is found and for whom the researcher gains new personalised information. We did not all know that our John Larkins Kensington was bankrupt in 1834!

Who will be interviewed about the family's history? Parents, grandparents, relations, genealogists in the family or knowledgeable family friends? Will this be face-to-face or through assists such as Facetime or Skype? In which ways will researchers make records of interviews? Can they use computer skills for this? Is there someone in the family or circle of friends who can assist? How will this family researcher clearly note follow-up research to be done by them or another family member? What responses will be noted as needing a follow-up in a subsequent interview?

Costing the Research Adventure

Costing estimates of this whole research adventure will be done prior to the first meeting. Consider the relatively high costs of joining the foremost family history research sites, buying materials for family members and records, family tree charts and display materials. Perhaps one of the extended family or an interested friend has a subscription to a prominent genealogical resource site and is happy to assist family members. Perhaps Ancestry is regarded as being used, at no cost, at the library. Perhaps some costs are shared across adult family members, especially for the cost of the four books that materially assist your family with their all-important internet searching. Each of the four has special merit and is worthy of purchase, especially if costs can be shared.

1. *The Family History Web Directory* by Jonathan Scott (Pen and Sword, 2015).
2. *The Genealogist's Internet* by Peter Christian (Bloomsbury, 2012).
3. *Tracing Your Family History on the Internet* by Chris Paton (Pen and Sword, 2013).
4. *Sharing Your Family History Online* by Chris Paton (Pen and Sword, 2021).

All are highly valued by family historians and very worthwhile for parents or researchers to purchase as they have a wide range of information, helpful lists of websites and internet sources for initial and wide-ranging research. Recommend these for purchase by your local library. Paton (2021) is an excellent contemporary publication and complements this present book's content by showing you how to take your research from you, and with you, into the internet world.

Practical Operational Considerations

Will you have an engaging family history display area in your home? Prepare for the establishment of an agreed workplace. This may be in a 'spare' room, in the study, in one part of a larger room, in an inviting basement area or conservatory room. It needs warmth, and space for displays, posters, ancestral charts, print resources and at-hand supplies of blank record forms. Will you have an 'Our Family History' whiteboard, or display area, for facts and queries? Perhaps below the display is a box for each researcher's new information, roadblocks and queries. Plan to make time for sharing each family member's findings or creations such as a weekly diary which draws upon the individual information boxes.

What will younger family members do to keep their records? What practical provisions of folders, files, notebooks and, say, five-generational charts, will you make available? What is kept online and what is kept in paper files? Consider the most computer adept researcher establishing a family blog. There are guides online. Will family members compile their records separately or will there be a central family storage site? Ensure all family members have ready access to the computer files and add to the family tree wall chart and timelines. Discuss backing up records with your family researchers to avoid technical obsolescence or power cuts with a resultant loss of stored family data. How will you develop free online file storage? This is where your search engine use is so rewarding.

Plan to share with grandparents and interested family members. Ask your computer savvy friends about the most appropriate aids for the research adventure. Where is their material best kept? Genealogist friends suggest aids such as Pages, Evernote, Microsoft OneNote, Dropbox or Google Docs to help with making the transition from paper notes to digital notes and/or storage. Are there computer skills in the family for storing and organising information? Are the youngsters familiar with how to download apps? Do they use Evernote for information storage, access Facebook, source blogs or utilise Flickr for their development of old photos and videos etc.?

Companies such as S&N Genealogy Supplies in England and Gould in Australia are mirrored in many countries as suppliers of research materials, ranging from charts to CDs and DVDs of specific fields of research, including ancient books of arms, heraldry, wills and historical county records. Use your search engines. Check magazines for free articles and record forms and get their free newsletters. Check genealogical book publishers. Pen and Sword, for example, are excellent with their range of county research books and books on specific sectors of genealogy. Unlock the Past books are functional, relatively basic, readable and inexpensive. It is interesting and informative to check genealogical materials and resources at sites such as National Archives. Locate, through search engines, family history publishers. Family history magazines sometimes provide helpful e-books to download, relatively inexpensively. How does your library select genealogical books and magazines, particularly those with a focus upon contemporary genealogical research?

Consider, in your immediate family, which child or young family member has certain interests or skills that would be of direct use for them in researching their family history. Do they know their parents' and grandparents' life histories? Do you know where your own parents grew up, began their careers, lived and met? Do you know your parents' hobbies, sports and special interests over time? Do you know their memories of their parents and grandparents?

Have you ever talked with your parents and grandparents about their growing up and life, some fifty years ago? Talk with your parents and older generation family members about their lives and their knowledge of their ancestors. Take notes, print them off and ask the subject(s) to check your record.

The goal of a family teenager might be to learn about the basic details of their direct ancestral line over five generations. The objectives would then become: to learn these ancestors' full names, births, marriages and deaths; to search newspapers for information on these ancestors; to interview parents and grandparents about these ancestors; and to research particular interests, such as in music, fashion, the military or voluntary public service, related to these ancestors.

Generating such interest will result from a well-planned first discussion. Be realistic about the effort required for planning this first meeting. Consider having a family quiz on your family's history. Ensure that you have a broad balance of both sides of your family – maternal and paternal.

Involvement of Others

Is there a close family friend, adult sibling of a parent or another family member, who might wish to develop their family's research as shared or parallel research? Are there cousins, to whom the family youngsters relate well, who could be interested? Consider how to involve each of the family, including parents, grandparents and extended family members. Indeed, the family's research adventure may be led by grandparents rather than parents.

The grandparents will be advised to plan for interviews from young members of the family. Explain the research venture to them and the probable enquiries that will come from their grandchildren. Ask them to sort out relevant memorabilia, documents and family photographs with information on these, giving their origin, associated family names, times and places.

Checklist of Preparation for the Family History Gathering

As strongly suggested earlier, consider, for your first family gathering, how you best approach this project as an innovative all-in family activity. What will appeal to individuals? Consider the following elements for this upcoming critical and innovative family time and why it should have a morning put aside for this.

1. Explain why we are doing this.
2. Do both parents have a clear sense and vision of the family team moving forward, collectively and individually, and of the mission, goals and processes to fulfil this.
3. Explain the parents have an initial goal of researching four, or perhaps five, generations.
4. Ensure clear understandings of what we want to find out.
5. List possible fields of research to follow up.
6. Have fun prizes for family knowledge games and puzzles.
7. Present a True or False quiz about past and present family members.
8. Provide jumbled surnames to be untangled.
9. Present a list of facts and ancestors to be matched.
10. Tell a few family stories.
11. Have questions about parents and grandparents.
12. Show samples of family memorabilia to be identified and explained.
13. Give out ancestor timelines and historical timelines to be linked and developed as research builds up.
14. Make some ancestors figures of excitement or special interest but avoid glorification.
15. Display a map of your country, with place names relevant in your family history.
16. Have a map of the world, with locations and names of ancestors to be placed onto it.
17. Provide brief family trees to provide starter information for each person.

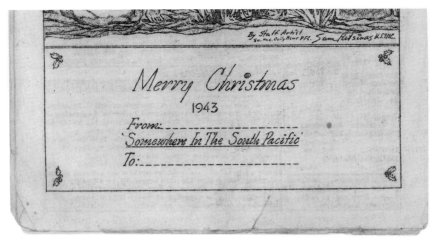

A father's Christmas card format when on active service in the Pacific.

18. Discuss possible team member pairings for engaging activities.
19. Ensure the participants have sufficient online access, notebooks and recording sheets.
20. Ensure space and research opportunity work together.
21. Preparation of grandparents for the enterprise.
22. Being aware of how this enterprise will be an *adventure*.
23. Planning for energising interest and participation from each family member.
24. Utilising visual impact – of photographs, of questions to solve, of charts of ancestral lines with highlighted gaps, queries and notes.
25. Making this first family get-together engaging and stimulating in an appropriate setting.
26. Having an enjoyable set of activities to foster family members' interest in family history.
27. Understand how this venture fits family time. If you are parents undertaking this research stimulus then ensure that each of you has a broadly equal contributing role in the first meeting.
28. Emphasising the range of domains of family history that family members could pursue as family history research is interlocked with a range of social and historical perspectives.
29. Seeking to share costs with members of the wider family to join at least two of the major research sites, such as Ancestry, Findmypast, TheGenealogist or MyHeritage and, certainly, the free and massive FamilySearch. Do check their records lists, options and categories. Learn how to save your finds on the website. All in the family can access these.

30. Ensuring that each family member will be able to handle the research activity they pursue and will feel valued by all the family team.
31. Having a possible time frame for the venture.

The tenor of the first family gathering will be critical. If you believe there is more likelihood of project acceptance by initially meeting individually with family members to discuss the family initiative, you should consider that. However, the full family session, with challenges, facts to follow up, guidance on initial research and the matching of possible research to certain family members is vital for family unity. In blatant terms, this family project is something you are 'selling' to the family team so target them sensitively and with a real awareness of what will appeal to them. Lead your family team with vision and realities.

Coping with Youngsters' Doubts

Some family leaders find youngsters have initial doubts, unwillingness and a lack of interest in the proposed family venture. This could be because they do not sense its personal relevance. Prepare for possible reactions from youngsters such as in the following examples.

1. 'I would rather be on my computer.'

   'That is great, Sam, because we will really need your help using your computer skills to do some of our research.'

2. 'Family history is boring, they're all dead anyway.'

   'Hey, you are very much alive and you are a very special part of our family's history. Let me explain ... '

3. 'What do you mean, that our present will one day be our past?'

   'Imagine, Sandy, when your grandparents' grandparents were alive. They would not have realised that, in later years, those *present* days of theirs would become our *past* days and part of our family's future days. The future members of our family will look back on these present days of yours as being in their past.'

4. 'How can we find out anything about our ancestors?'

   'That is such a good question, and I don't know all of the answers! I have had to begin by myself, but I did learn a lot! I can help you with the best ways to start and you are smart enough to follow on from there. You know I am ready to help at any time.'

5. 'I think it's boring. I would rather find out about sport!'

'Chris, I'm pleased you said that. You can do just that! We do not know a lot about what sports our family played this century and last century. Perhaps we start with you and your brothers and sister and then you interview your parents and grandparents to find out what sports they played and where? Look closely at what you might like to find out about sports played by our ancestors. You might like to collect photographs that illustrate what you find out and then share them. We are sure you could make a timeline.'

Sport as an Example of Family History Interest

Typical starting questions are readily adaptable for any of the areas of individual or paired interest held by your younger family. The family history of sport engagement is an example which could readily be applied to any strong family member interest.

1. Does anyone in the family know of the sports played by our ancestors?
2. Where were they living? When was this?
3. Did your grandparents play sport at school, at home or for a club? What did their parents and grandparents play? How do we know?
4. What sports did boys play? What sports did girls play? Did girls have the same opportunities to play sport? If not, why not?
5. Did anyone in our family collect autographs or write to sports people?
6. Did anyone ever qualify as a coach?
7. Do we have any photographs of any of our sporting ancestors? Would Grandma and Grandpa have any?
8. Do you have any photographs of mum or dad and sport?
9. If I give you the names and key dates of past family members, could you find out the sports that were played where they lived?
10. Are there any histories of their towns which mention sports there?
11. Can we locate photographs in local archives or sport bodies?
12. Does any high school attended by my parents or grandparents or great-grandparents have sport team photographs in their library, assembly hall, changing rooms, hallways or elsewhere?

COLLECTING CRICKETERS' AUTOGRAPHS.

I have been collecting autographs for almost eighteen months now.   We
have a lot that my father collected when he was a boy including
autographs of Sir Donald Bradman, Sir Leon Hutton, Frank Woolley,
Wilfred Rhodes and many other players and teams.

I love cricket and get autographs by asking cricketers or by writing
away.   I like showing them to my friends and keep them in my
autograph book or up on my wall.   When someone you like as a cricketer
has written his name down you almost feel as if you know him.   They
are special because they are personal I think.

You have to plan ahead and see what games are on and what the playing
hours are.   Then you can go to the ground before the day's play.   If
I write away I put return postage in with my letter asking for the
autograph.   I especially enjoy getting team autographs.   My favourite
team's autographs were in a letter I received from the 1981-2 Australian
team in New Zealand which I was sent with a note from the manager, Mr.
Crompton.

My favourite single autographs are Sir Donald Bradman's and Geoffrey
Boycott's.   We have a letter and photograph from Sir Donald which means
a lot to me because I have read such a lot about him.   I hoped to get
Geoffrey Boycott's autographed picture for my birthday and sent off a
British Postal Note for the postage.   He sent me an autographed
photograph and returned the money.   He wrote in the envelope to tell
me that my letter got forwarded to him too late to get back in time for
my birthday.

If you get the autograph or autographed picture of someone you like to
know more about the cricketer whose autograph you have.   I usually browse
or read in 'The Cricketer' or 'Cricket Player' or 'Wisden Cricket Monthly'
or books or Wisden.

Christopher (Kit) McConnell - 9yrs.

A 9-year-old family member drafts a cricket article.

13. Can I write to a school and ask them about one of our family playing
    sport there?
14. Did your ancestors play with any famous players or have especially
    favourite teams or sports people?
15. How could you use online searches to find out more?
16. Your ancestors were overseas in the First World War and the Second
    World War. Did they play sport at all?
17. You know that your great-grandfather was in a prisoner of war camp
    for a short time. You could find out if he played any sports there.

18. Could we work together and make a sport history timeline (or timeline of your favourite sport) and find out any ancestors who fit the sport timeline?

19. You could use Google to see if an ancestor, a family place and sport fit together. I can help you learn to search newspapers because they often have club teams and local match reports of your ancestor's time.

20. Often a workplace had a sport team – can we check on this? Was any ancestor a sponsor of a sport team? How could you learn about these? Would you write to the factory where your great-grandfather worked?

21. Did any female ancestor play sport? Consider tennis, croquet, lacrosse, netball and basketball and swimming.

22. The branches of our family that migrated may have played sport on their ship. Where on the ship would they have played this? What would they have played? Can we find shipboard diaries or reports of this? Did grandparents travel overseas by boat, as tourists, and play sport on board?

23. Did ancestors play different sports in their new homeland?

Puna Taua in Epsom Girls' Grammar hockey team.

24. Has anyone been involved in coaching, fitness, dietary or medical roles with a sport?

25. Was any direct or collateral ancestor a sports reporter, writer or commentator?

26. Was any ancestor a referee or umpire?

27. How did sports clothing and equipment change over the years?

28. Is there anyone living who played sport with your parent or grandparent?

29. Are there any family scrapbooks, letters, diaries, school reports or awards that were my ancestor's?

30. Research to find out if any ancestors were selected for special events or were awarded cups, medals or trophies individually or as a team member.

31. How did sports gear, equipment and clothing change from an ancestor's day to the present?

A grammar school XV inter-school rugby game, with one direct line participant.

32. It is important for later family members to know about sport in our present-day family as it tells them about us and about our family life. Could you record what sports you are playing and why you play those sports? What would a future generation wish to know about today's family and their sport?

Find resources such as Hicks (2015) and Brasch (1995) which can assist you to compile your sport history timeline. You could use search engines to find articles about carrying out family history and sport history research together.

An example of searching is the range of sport media resources related to individual biographies, participation, obituaries, competition or match reports in local newspaper and school reports through to participation at regional and national levels. What could the *Ulster Football and Cycling News*, which began in 1887 as the *Ulster Cyclist and Football News*, tell us about sports and forebears in that place and time? Check the British Newspaper Archive.

Professional sport is generally well served. Cricket, for example, has Lillywhite's annual publication and the Wisden cricket almanacs, which began in 1849 and 1864 respectively. Imagine the surprise if Toby is sitting in the library to check family surnames in the *Wisden Book of Obituaries* (Green, 1986) and finds Henry Maturin (1842–1920). The entry reveals that Maturin was a fast round-arm bowler. He played village cricket into his seventies and played in one game when the team had fourteen players. Is he a relation? Toby will find, in an online search of Ancestry family trees, that he and Henry Maturin do share a Maturin ancestor. Toby will also learn about two aspects of his favourite sport that he did not know before – round-arm bowling and occasional teams of fourteen players. On a different level, Toby could obtain a scrapbook of sport newspaper clippings and school yearbook entries about one of his grandfathers, handed down by his great-grandmother.

The above is provided to reinforce the potential for researching a path with a special family interest. If Toby had been researching clothing or farming, the path above would have been similar. Consider following through on a youngster's strong interest in entertainment, handcraft, music, cooking, dance, armed services, education, studies, or fashion. A similar exploration could be done with interests such as farming, hobbies, fitness and community groups such as Girl Guides, Scouts and Girls' and Boys' Brigades. Virtually all the questions in the above sport list could be adapted to fit another interest to explore or trigger part of the youngster's account of life in the family's past and in the present.

Understand young family members' unique perspectives on what a family is and what they would wish to explore. Consider this simple question for your younger family members: 'What would you ask your ancestors about their lives so their answers would help us understand how they lived?' The answers to this question usually offer real-life insights beyond those of us who are simply content with recording birth, marriage and death records.

One youngster had a strong interest in weather extremities, having been aware of a tornado. He compiled newspaper accounts that outlined weather disasters in areas where ancestors had lived then had the enterprise to search newspapers of the time to locate first-hand accounts of the weather's disastrous impact upon a forerunner's farm crops. Two of these reports mentioned ancestors of the family researcher.

Be wary of over-emphasising the standard research lines of family trees and core genealogical research sites. Why not allow the youngster to come into the family research with a sense of personal adventure? This can often develop from their special interests to be followed. These could help in framing interview questions for parents and grandparents or be researched as possible areas of change in past and present family life. Invariably, they will search the standard sites and family trees. Be prepared with family interest choices that could be searched through time, such as in the following fields:

- Arts and crafts
- Books and reading interests
- Cooking

- Education and learning
- Fashion and clothes
- Games, indoors and outdoors
- Gardening
- Health
- Hobbies
- Home appliances and utensils
- Home machinery
- Homes lived in
- Languages learned
- Leisure time
- Lifelong learning
- Migration
- Military Service
- Musical interests
- Occupations
- Other cultures
- Pets
- Photographs and portraits
- Recreation and games
- Religion
- Rural life and farming
- Schools and further education
- Science
- Sport
- Tools and carpentry equipment
- Town life
- Toys
- Transport modes
- Travel
- Volunteer and community organisations
- Wars and military history

What might appeal to individual family members? Any of the above can lead to a series of research explorations that can add to the present-day family's records for the future family. For example, one of your family may have a special interest in clothes and fashion. That can easily lead to similar considerations as noted for family sport. See Chapter 6.

Toys and games excite some young family members as a focus for research. What toys did different generations prize? Can parents and grandparents tell us more? This is often engaging for a younger person moving back through their family history. This may well prove to be initially challenging but can readily be supported by research and be their path into a wider understanding of the family's history. See Henderson (2018) and the books on toys and games over time. These endeavours reinforce family cohesion through enjoyable mutual research.

Researching Women in the Family

One family member, who strongly developed an interest in women's rights and the changes of women's roles in home and society, had an aunt's assistance to compile a women's history timeline and a family history timeline. She discovered conventions imposed upon her female ancestors by society's laws and assumptions, that women in distaff lines did not have equality, in social, civic and legal contexts, with men. This knowledge deepened when the youngster found her great-great-grandmothers were absent were absent in early electoral rolls etc. and found that women were noted with subservient language or categorisations and, historically, even absent as they did not have the rights (e.g. to vote) that men had.

Expanding her research, she noted such aspects as: women in family history standing for office or being restricted in doing so; role expectations; independence; occupational expectations and restrictions; political movements; societal status and societal expectations; marriage rights; compound difficulties of being a woman of colour; legal rights; names and nomenclature for women and men; changing levels of sport equity; educational opportunities for certain careers and political impositions and opportunities. From her grandparents, the young woman researcher learned of her great-great-great grandmother's involvement in the suffragette movement. Then the search began for newspaper mentions and petitions.

To enhance youngsters' understanding of their predecessors' lives, you could locate 'old-time' tourist venues or museums which have exhibits and activities that will be informative and engaging on a family visit: 'See that iron machine? When I was a child, that was exactly the sort of plough that my grandpa's draught-horses had to pull.'

In your family there may be children who have not yet developed research skills with computers. We have adopted a definition of family history that supports youngsters playing significant roles in developing the records of their family in the present – to pass into the future. Diaries can be written or drawn; memorabilia compiled; photographs taken of people; copies made of awards and certificates; records made of the family home; artwork created to pass on to later generations; creative and factual writing can be done; and local newspaper and club publications searched. Interviews of the younger family members could be carried out by each other, by older siblings, parents, grandparents or done as self-interviews. These would be recorded with names and dates and could cover aspects of daily life, school, leisure time, home, work and play, favourite possessions, hobbies, whole-family activities, siblings, parents and grandparents. Check the possible topics listed above as they provide aspects of life today that the youngster may wish to write about for the future family. These are discussed further in Chapter 7 and could go into the time capsule discussed in Chapter 10.

You may wish to invite other family members, particularly grandparents, to this first 'setting the scene' meeting. If so, do prepare them with a full understanding of how you see family history and expected family member contributions. Do explain to grandparents their indispensable roles in the research and likely lines of investigation that family members may pursue with them. Two pieces of memorabilia could be brought by them and explained.

Family Session Targets and Follow-Ups

There should be agreed goals, individual and communal, for the first phase of the family's project. Consider having a target date for completion of the research resulting from this coming meeting. This future date could recognise each family member presenting their findings, interviews and results to the family within the timeframe. When that day arrives, invite key members of the extended family to be there. Make this special! Ensure each family researcher is commended for their involvement and attitude. Participation after this follow-up time would be completely voluntary.

Avoid indicating there will be what others may consider as overly frequent family team meetings. Provide core materials for filing recorded interviews. Perhaps you will make the occasional full family research get-togethers an enjoyable and special time, with a special meal or treat of favoured takeaways or drink and cakes!

A critical dimension of success in family history research, whether done individually or cooperatively, is the recording of the process and its results. Be prepared. Can your family participants use an aid such as Evernote, Flickr or Calibre? Some researchers find it valuable to have research records on a spreadsheet for cumulative lists of searches and findings. Integral to this is the storage plan to record what research was done, the findings (or lack of findings), the placement of results in assigned files and notes designating follow-up to be done.

File boxes are easy to use with all material on a certain family surname located in them, including birth, marriage and death records and the related conglomeration of extracts, notes, certificates, printed results, photocopied material etc. Have subsets of folders for specific ancestors and collateral ancestors with that surname. Will each family member retain their own record of *their* research processes and findings or non-findings or will they contribute these to the family file box? As research expands you will need online storage. Explore this early on. Virtually all genealogical researchers place results in online locations. This becomes a key consideration as results mount up, material is increasing and online storage looms invitingly. Use your search engine or skilled friends' advice to check out this process. Learn about GEDCOM and placing files online and sharing trees. (See, for example, in the bibliography, Crume (Undated) and Morton (2021)). Many organised genealogists use such assistance as Dropbox or Evernote.

Summary

In summary, the planning for your first family meeting on researching the family's history has included practical research considerations. These will be drawn together under the convenor's overall goals for this forthcoming family history research period. It will reflect the beliefs that you, the family leaders, do have a basic knowledge of how to research family history; that you consider your family as a team not a group and appreciate that each family team member has a valued role in this research adventure. What will each member enjoy researching? How do you best coach your children in this? You will take into this critical half-day of family research planning a sound set of preparations.

Throughout this forthcoming new family development your young family members need to understand and accept that they are part of their family history at present, in their ongoing lives. They need to understand they are key persons in the cross-generational story of the family they are now learning about. Young and old family members will find pleasure passing on family history to future generations. What will each family member be able to do? Plan for optional paired participation in the research. The riches each family member can bring to the family history adventure will, in turn, bring a new richness to the family, present and future.

Be selective. Be realistic. Be practical. Be encouraging. Be caring. Do not rush into the meeting or overload the family. This is an initiation day for what is a potentially engrossing family adventure. You have carried out basic research to enable you to confidently provide guidance and material for the family. You are clear about the key aspects of family history, how these will be researched by family members individually and collectively, the elements that make researching family history exciting and intriguing and how the results will be organised and passed on. It is vital that the parents, or grandparents, or others in the family carrying out the leadership roles, feel wholly prepared. If this is so, we can now consider the whole family team stepping forward for this major time together, launching the researching of their own family history.

Chapter 3

YOUR FAMILY RESEARCH GATHERING

The First Meeting

You have prepared well. You have established a congenial setting. You have a clear idea of how to approach this first gathering and how each family member can be involved. The key materials are ready and accessible. Approach this family gathering in such a way as to make it a 'Finding Out Who We Are' research adventure. Emphasise the elements of pleasure and discovery.

For this first gathering have a clear idea of how you plan your time. Explain your interest in family history and its research. Emphasise, from the start, the pleasure of undertaking challenging research like a family detective. This is the unique opportunity for young family members to engage in the presentation of their lives today to be passed on to their descendants of tomorrow. You could show a range of family tree charts and tell of some intriguing ancestors and their links with history or unusual happenings. Discuss possible ways the research can be organised and how everyone's findings will be integrated, for their own knowledge and pleasure and for later generations.

You might wish to start with previously noted quizzes etc. that you now implement, with fun prizes, to be enjoyed by the family. Engage everyone in these quizzes, which you have prepared to stimulate their interest in ancestors. One family was stimulated by the 'Discover Your Ancestor' board game their parents constructed. One pair of more extrovert parents enacted a historical interview with an ancestor and acted it out. Explain the 'something for everyone' belief for a whole-family research approach. Explain the definition that underpins the family history: *family history is a history of the direct family in the past and in the present – recorded for the future.* Explain how this places importance upon each present family member, their opportunities to research the family's past and their contribution to 'record for the future'. The youngest will contribute more fully to the latter aspect. Explain the exploration upon which all are embarking – parents, grandparents and children – individually and collectively.

There are immediate reassurances needed for family members. They have computer or other skills – if not they will be initially guided with these. They can write, draw, compose, or photograph. They use social media. They are imaginative and resourceful. They will be helped with whatever they choose and they will hand on understandings of themselves to future generations. Do explain the various fields of special interest research, noted in the previous chapter, they may wish to follow. Have the young ones ask for whatever they feel is needed for their art, handcraft, writing, photography, drawings and diary of a week. Draw upon the research guide sources you have assembled and now distribute these.

Memorabilia

Have some selected family memorabilia and explain their relevance. Perhaps grandparents could talk about some of these. They could be selected from a range of special possessions:

- Art pieces
- Awards and church records
- Certificates
- Cookbooks / recipes
- Craft works
- Cutlery
- Diaries, notebooks and journals.
- Documents
- Furnishings
- Degrees
- Handcrafts
- Hand-me-down creations or objects
- Heirlooms
- Inscriptions in books
- Knitting or crochet pieces, wall hangings, embroidery, quilts
- Letters and cards
- Newspaper articles
- Occupational qualifications
- Ornaments

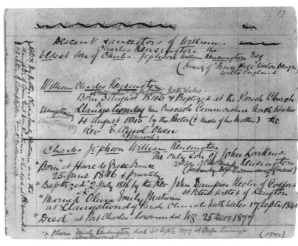

A handwritten extract from William Charles Kensington's notebook.

Queen Elizabeth award of Her Majesty's Silver Jubilee Medal 6 February 1977 to Norma McConnell (née Kensington).

- Paintings and miniatures.
- Photographs and videos
- School reports
- Souvenirs
- Toys and games
- Woodwork tools

Charles Kensington (1749–1807) married Louisa de la Porte 1773. (Engleheart miniaturist).

It is easy to imagine the memorabilia meaning of quilts made by Jayne for each of her four children and the family treasure of quilts made by Lorraine for her five children. Jayne created a beautiful embroidery when the author and Puna married. This has key dates on it. She also did a valued drawing of their farm. These need to be written about by the recipients so their depth of meaning is passed on to later generations.

In 2021, Jayne began original oil paintings of her siblings' grandchildren. They are remarkable in their recognition of each child and quality of the art. (Any family could consider similar present-day art, photography, handwork gifts or portrayals that would become prized by their recipients and descendants.)

My father contracted malaria while serving in the Royal New Zealand Air Force in the Pacific in the Second World War. In New Caledonia Hospital, for his malaria therapy, he compiled beautiful leather writing compendiums, model planes and a carefully crafted fruit bowl from crashed aeroplane materials, now with his granddaughter. Consider the 1891 mother-of-pearl piece from Isabella Coleman, the valiant missionary in China, which has come down to the author's daughter.

An 10-year-old, Sophia, will one day have *Prester John*, which was inscribed by her great-grandmother in Form IV (second year of high school) in 1930, and Maya, Cleo, Sophia and Toby, each have a set of seven books, written by their grandfather, appropriately inscribed to them. It is important to record which family members receive, now or in the future, any of the family memorabilia.

Rare and special memorabilia are, advisedly, listed in a will. Other important family artefacts could be discussed with family members and a clear list of these, with their future recipients, should be made for each family member. With each item should be an account of its origin and family meaning.

Have an enjoyable time now with the photographs you have previously assembled. The project is a great time for sorting out family photographs and naming people in them. There could be copies made for

The sport one of the family loved but grandchildren never identified with.

each family member. Explain the possible enhancement of these without distorting them. Try and place them in chronological order. Put names and dates on the back, where these are known. Children will ask, 'Who are they? How am I related to them?' Are there any discernible facial features of ancestors? Two outdoor photographs stimulated conjecture in children and grandchildren. 'Is that Uncle Kit in the rugby team?' 'We don't know who this is. We don't think it's really our grandfather because he would never, ever, do water-skiing!'

Tasks and Their Challenges

It is easy for a family, undertaking mutual research and stimulating individual research, to become a little overwhelmed by the whole-family adventure. Be alert to this. Do not overload family members. Do not immediately plan for necessarily searching ancestors of long ago but with a goal of researching, say, five generations. Each individual ancestor should be numbered (as on the family tree chart) so the number can become their 'ID' and obviate potential errors. Colour coding could be used for family surnames. Younger family members can develop their own family ancestry charts or draw up family trees and enter ancestors' names with their births, marriages and deaths.

Outline individual tasks that could be undertaken and discuss who will undertake these. Have clear facets of the research experience for children and older members of the family to consider. Make these interesting, exciting and, especially, realistic and attainable. Fasten on to whichever interest, idea, question, challenge or skill might result in enthusiasm for interests your children wish to pursue. Will Mollie and her cousin, Bhodi, each have the same stimulus? One might wish to learn more about their ancestry, the next could be stimulated by using computer skills and one might want to find out about an ancestor involved in 'real history'. What if Tauren and Tilly over-estimate their research skills? What if a couple of siblings, Annah and Kyla, might like to research together?

In another family group we could find Lexie, Ari and Enzo becoming enthusiastic at being able to tell the family of previously unknown achievements of an ancestor and Sienna, the youngest, might like to keep a weekly diary (written or drawn) to put away for future family members to read. Ryleigh, the teenager, will probably see herself starting a family blog. Ensure a buy-in from them with an assurance and explanation of your support for them and your enjoyment of helping at any stage.

The most valuable in-family sources will be family members. Interviewing grandparents or other older generation family members can have the golden impact of them being valued and often results in them writing down information to give to the grandchildren – not only about themselves but about their parents or grandparents, and how the family came to their present location.

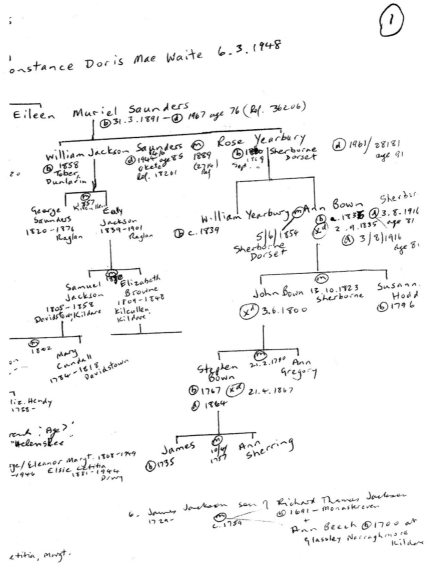

Part of the work-in-hand Waite family tree.

You may have a family member who will enjoy a focus upon assembling birth, marriage and death dates and relevant information such as a newspaper obituary. They might wish to photograph related tombstones and make these available to distant and future family members.

You will be guiding the family into readily available major research bases. Help them understand how to note their sources, establish clear files and number individuals (using numbers from the family tree chart) and colour-code groups for those who share an ancestor. In using record sheets for their searches there is a simple logic with each search that helps to keep the search informative and replicable.

1. The purpose of the search e.g. to find a birth, marriage, death certificate.
2. The date the search was performed.
3. The specific search e.g. 'Ancestry family trees for William Yearbury married Ann Bown 1854'.
4. A summary of what was or was not found in this specific search.
5. What to follow up on e.g. 'No trace, I shall check Yearbury of Dorset in a census'.
6. Sharing results and knowledge of new sites.
7. Noting unexpected possibilities for further research.
8. Questions to share in order to obtain suggestions for a possible follow-up.

DNA

Check out DNA testing if you have not done this or had tests done. It would be helpful to have the tests done for each parent, and grandparent. The older family members will be intrigued by the results and the DNA test firm sending emails to you, over time, listing probable relatives, who may be previously unknown but whom you can usually contact. Different researchers have different goals, whether finding missing relatives, a desire to locate more knowledge of ancestors, learning about ethnic orientations, health interests or gaining knowledge of broad geographic linkages. Which test will you take? A common purpose is to have an autosomal test as that is a broad starting point of your DNA researching. Utilise search engines. Check Ancestry, 23AndMe and MyHeritage.

Our family has found the DNA matching, which gives the names of others showing genetic links with you, to be very appealing. However, do remember that DNA tests can result in unexpected and even upsetting results. (See Appendix 2.)

There are excellent explanations and evaluations of DNA services in a range of accessible sites. Sites such as 23AndMe, Ancestry and My Heritage should be checked out. A range of genealogical sites provide assessments of DNA suppliers. Ancestry is deemed to have the biggest database of tests done and is reputable. 23andMe is a major test organisation database. MyHeritage allows genealogists to freely load DNAs obtained from other sites onto this site. Check other sites to learn where your DNA can be lodged. Wikitrees is liked by genealogists because it has a collection of millions of ancestor profiles and a large integration of DNA data. See also such sites as DNA help for Genealogy (UK) and the YouTube tutorial on **www.irishorigenes.com** and **www.madaboutgenealogy.com** where information and queries are shared. Family history magazines, noted in Appendix 1, often have helpful articles.

Ensure someone in your circle of family and friends understands the DNA results – what they show and what they do not. Family historians often have their DNA tested by more than one company. Your extended family may have someone, or know of someone, who can explain new terminology to you. See Chapter 5 of Paton (2021).

Familiarise your family with the two helpful timelines you originally constructed, with copies for each family member. One timeline formulates historical events and significant dates in history and the other is populated with your family history dates, such as births, deaths, marriages, migration dates, military appointments, major purchases such as farms and ancestor events found in historical newspapers. Plan specific challenges for specific youngsters to find significant dates and periods. One family found that when they provided copies to grandparents and supportive aunts and uncles these resulted in new information on family persons who had particular links with the timeline content.

Moving Past the First Meeting

The parents or other leaders have developed a core knowledge of initial research sites and have five-generation family tree charts with known dates and names inscribed. Careful thought has gone into how the research will be seen as an adventure by family members and notebooks have been obtained. Online access is readily available. Individuals have been motivated. They have a broad understanding of family history challenges and specific aspects to pursue as they are now familiar with methods of following through on initial research.

Consider the resultant work that will need one-on-one sessions with individual family members. This should be done more supportively than correctively. In accord with the concept that *family history is a history of the direct family in the past and in the present – recorded for the future*, sensitive attention will have been given to how the younger family members contribute their perception and recording of themselves and their family in the present.

A ready example is the Covid-19 pandemic. The author's grandchildren mentioned that, having moved through part of the Coronavirus pandemic in lockdown, they would be interested to learn about the Spanish Flu that was estimated to cause the infection of up to one-third of the world's population in 1918–1920. These grandchildren of today could leave interesting family history accounts of their lives during the Coronavirus pandemic, perhaps with diary extracts, drawings and newspaper articles. Intra-family and inter-family emails, cards and interviews would add to the impact of these prized family history records. Your youngsters may wish to leave masks in their family time capsule.

Plan a subsequent follow-up family meeting, which will include enjoyable feedback, updates on findings and probably presentations. One note of caution – do not make this research adventure an endless all-in family endeavour. Consider the initial family research adventure as Phase One. That is the key time of primary stimulation, activation, challenges and excitement – concomitant with the motivation of individual family member research activities and the location of new information.

Phase One might be the complete extent of some family members' involvement. There is no compulsion on anyone to undertake what could be termed as Phase Two. That phase will be over to the follow-through of individual family members pursuing their own interests and challenges in continuing their family history research. Whatever 'Phase Two' journey your family members are embarking upon, collectively and individually, they will continue on their own terms.

Chapter 4

USING YOUR IN-FAMILY SOURCES

Parents, grandparents, aunts and uncles, family members who have done some research, or close family friends, can be the first interviewees by your team members. Their information will be the basis of researchers following into online sites.

Family history is a positive force of well-being for elderly persons and, perhaps especially, for those with dementia. A Speech and Language Pathologist, working with dementia patients, notes strongly that, 'Giving someone with dementia the opportunity to tell their 'story' is a key in maintaining their sense of self and identity' (p.70, Lima, 2019). This is a significant underscoring and reassurance of what you will be doing as a leader of this venture.

Interviewing well is a challenging experience that takes practice. Help young researchers outline their research processes, questions and recording materials. Someone may prefer not to be engaged in interviews and to be the family's present-day recorder who draws upon findings and updates family timeline details of happenings, special days, emigration, anniversaries, birthdays etc. The records could include duplicates of family interviews. Consider resources they may need.

Interviews of Grandparents

Ensure sound preparation for all interviews. What do we *want* to know? What do we *need* to know? How will the interview be recorded? Is technical guidance needed? Younger family members should have a range of proposed questions and not have a complete list imposed upon them. Teach them how to interview, with guidance for them emphasising the careful selection of priority questions and interview skills.

- To be relaxing and confident in recording.
- To have sound planning of the setting and time.
- Using questions of their own and from this chapter.
- Perhaps have an interview rehearsal.
- Learn how to draw out a brief answer if more information is sought.
- Check with the interviewee on any answer not understood or which, in your view, is incomplete or unclear or does not give the information you are seeking.
- Making notes or transposing the interview recording immediately after interviewing.
- Thanking the interviewees.

Interviews need a quiet space. Grandparents may choose not to answer some questions. They must be asked about recording the interview. Interviewers could ask their grandparents if they, the interviewees, would rather not participate orally but would be willing to write answers to the questions. This has the positive side of the older generation having time to reflect, think of illustrative replies and discuss their replies with each other. Questions from the following list could be selected for a range of interviews:

1. What are your full names?
2. When and where you were born? Why were you living there?
3. What are your earliest memories?
4. Where did you each live and grow up?
5. What are your siblings' full names? When and where were they born?
6. What was your surname, Nana, before you were married?
7. Do you know how and why you were given your names?
8. What were your mothers' surnames before they each married?
9. Do you each know your grandmothers' surnames before they married?
10. Who was the eldest family person you knew? What can you tell us about them?
11. What did you do in your spare time when you were young? Did you have huts or hideaways or play areas?
12. Can you describe the district or neighbourhood in which you grew up?
13. Could you tell us about pets you had? What were they, who got them, who named them? What were their names?
14. What were your favourite toys and favourite indoor and outdoor games?

15. What special memories do you have of family life, family activities, the weekends, religious life, work, travel or holidays?
16. Who did you ever go and stay with? Why? Where did they live? How did you get there?
17. Can you remember first getting a TV or refrigerator or radio or computer or a takeaway meal?
18. What did you listen to on the radio?
19. What did you want to be when you grew up?
20. How did you both meet?
21. When did you marry? Where? Please tell me about your wedding day. Do you have photographs of the day? Can you tell us who is in the photo?
22. Can you tell us about our parents' wedding day?
23. Did your parents ever tell you about their parents and grandparents and their lives? If so, what did they tell you? Can you give us an outline of their lives?
24. Do you know of any important dates in your grandparents' lives, such as when they were born or married or died?
25. Where did they live? Where are they buried?
26. Are there any stories or memories about your parents you can share?
27. What were their full names?
28. Where did your parents grow up?
29. How did your parents meet?
30. What are special memories you have of your parents?
31. How did your grandparents meet?
32. Are there any stories or memories about your grandparents you can share?
33. What are special memories you have of your grandparents?
34. When young, did you spend time with them? What did you do?
35. Did you have a favourite doll or toy?
36. What did you eat for meals when you were young? Did your family have takeaways?
37. Did you have a vegetable garden and/or fruit trees? If so, who looked after these?
38. Could you describe each of your grandparents?
39. What favourite memories do you have of your mother?
40. What favourite memories do you have of your father?
41. What were the names of your brothers and sisters? Can you tell us about them?
42. Did you love having children? What appealed (or did not appeal) to you?

43. What were special days you celebrated in your life as a child and as an adult? Why were they special?
44. How did you celebrate birthdays and Christmas?
45. Were there other special days in your year? What were they?
46. Tell us about times when your family were all doing something together.
47. What household things did you have that we do not have or use now?
48. What rooms were in your home? Who had their own bedroom?
49. Can you tell us the locations of any homes where our ancestors, lived?
50. What schools did you go to? What did you like or not like about school? What were your favourite subjects? Were there subjects that we do not have at school now? What are they? Why, do you think, they stopped being taught? How were pupils punished and for what were they punished?
51. Did you ever have a nickname? How did that come about?
52. Did you belong to clubs or play sport or dance? If so, what were these?
53. Please tell us about your high school years: school subjects you excelled at and struggled with, sports and activities, jobs, friends, dates, learning to drive, how you got along with your parents.
54. What were your favourite sports to play (or watch) when young, your hobbies and activities inside and outside the home? Did you collect anything?
55. Were you ever naughty? If so, what did you do? What happened as a result?
56. What career did you have? Why did you choose that? How did you train for that?
57. Did you get any qualifications or career certificates?
58. Could you tell us about the jobs you have had and how you got into each one?
59. Where did you settle as an adult? Why did you choose that place?
60. When you were an adult, who were your friends? How did those friendships develop? Who have been your best friends? Why did you like them so much? Did you keep school friends after you left school?
61. Do you have any certificates or printed family history information or memorabilia that you could show us and tell us about?
62. Is there any book that mentions an ancestor of ours?
63. What do you do in spare time? What games or hobbies or sport or music or dancing do you enjoy as an adult?

64. Do any family members live in a different country from ours? Who were they? Are you still in contact?
65. Do you have a favourite season? Why is it your favourite?
66. Have you had a DNA test? If you have that done or intend to have that done, would you share the results with us?
67. Can you talk us through all the homes you have lived in, why you chose them and why you left them?
68. Have you travelled overseas? Why did you go? Where did you go? Did you like travelling? Why? Did you have a favourite place overseas? Why did you like it?
69. Did you go to any of our family history places? If you did, what can you tell us?
70. What is your favourite part of our country? Why do you choose that?
71. As an older person now, how did you choose where you now live? How do you spend your days?
72. What are your main interests?
73. What do you think are the best things you have done?
74. Are there differences in technology today compared with your earlier years? What are they?
75. What has been your favourite music in your life? Why is this?
76. What were your favourite books? Why do you choose these?
77. How did you get to school and get home?
78. Are there any recipes that you would like to pass on to us?
79. Were you ever sick or in hospital?
80. What, would you say, is your hometown? What changes have taken place in your hometown in terms of shops, buildings and services? Why do you think this has happened?
81. Could you help us identify people in our older family photographs?
82. What do you wish your parents or grandparents had told you?
83. Would you help with a map of our country and a world map by placing names of ancestors on them at their locations?
84. What would you tell us, your grandchildren, about how to be happy and enjoy life and people? Can you give real-life examples from your lives?
85. Did you, or anyone in your family, have favourite sayings or lucky numbers?
86. Did your parents or grandparents pass any family stories on to you?
87. Is there anyone else in our family, or who is a family friend, who could help us learn more about our family? How could we contact them?

88. What are the most important things that you have learned about life that you would like to share with your grandchildren?
89. Are there any names that have been passed down through our family?
90. Are there any similarities between you and me? Do you see any similarities between mum or dad and me? What are they?
91. Would you please write out the family tree, for each of you, as far as you know it?
92. If there was one person to see again, with whom you have lost touch, who would that be? Why do you choose them? Where did they last live?
93. We will be passing on to future generations what we know of our ancestors, and how we live today. Are there any points we should make?
94. Are there any ancestors you think we should investigate so we can pass on that knowledge and share it with you when we find it?
95. Were there shops when you were young that we hardly ever see now?
96. Did we ever have a coat of arms? If so, where can we see a copy?
97. If our family belongs to a church how did that come about?
98. What do you think we should write about, describing family life today, that our descendants would find interesting?
99. If we wrote about how family coped with Covid-19 and lockdown what would you suggest we note for our descendants who would read about it?
100. When we grow up, what are the qualities you would value most in us as adults?
101. Do any in our extended family have family records, diaries, letters or special books?
102. Would you mind checking our record of this interview after we write it up?

More than 900 additional questions are available on Greene and Fulford (1993). Take some special action to thank your grandparents, such as a delivered gift or personal note. You could ask if you can give a record of the interview to your cousins. You might like to trace the 'lost' close friend(s) of the grandparents as a mode of thanking grandparents for their interviews participation. You could explore MyHeritage and FamilySearch apps to learn about setting your interviews on other tree profiles. Your family techno-star can explore these and other sites and should check Paton (2021) for excellent coverage of putting family history online.

You could undertake research that is novel for a family history – have the grandparents interview your family. They could draw upon the questions that were being asked of them, develop additional questions of their own and then interview their adult children and grandchildren. This provides a novel and usually exciting illustration of the second and third parts of our definition of family history: *family history is a history of the direct family in the past and in the present – recorded for the future.*

Write to aunts and uncles who are in your line of family history, know your family history or who can recall family members of a preceding generation. Also, consider discussions with those who are 'like family' and who are, or have been, close friends. Draw upon questions for grandparents noted above, subsequent trigger words and the following possible enquiries for such friends.

- What were your links with our family?
- How did you become friends with our family?
- Can you give us names of any family members we may not know?
- Can you tell us about a specific family member or happenings in their life?
- Can you tell us about any of our family homes? Where did our family live?

Schoolboy friends and neighbour friends – still in touch many decades later.

- Did you share any activities with our family? What were these?
- Do you have any family tree information on our family?
- Do you have any records, photographs or memorabilia of our family?
- Were there any family legends or stories associated with our family?
- Were there special days? How were these celebrated?
- What do you remember about childhood friends we could talk to?
- Who might tell us more?

Writing Your Personal Memoirs

The grandparent interview questions also work as prompts for family members to write their personal life stories for descendants. Plan this venture. The list of possibilities for discourse noted above can help with your writing a personal memoir. There is much of older generations' early life that still surprises our grandchildren. Consider radios we listened to, the lack of fast-food places, no mobile phone, very few takeaways except for fish shops, the cars we drove, getting to school, no television or iPad or computer, going to cinemas because there was no other source of movies to see, apart from some drive-ins. In the home there may have been no refrigerator, electric iron, indoor lavatory, dishwasher, washing machine, electric shaver or electric tools. Could your children believe their grandparents stood for the national anthem before the cinema movie began? There are many ideas online for writing a personal history, but a simple guide would include the following:

- Think of the purpose of your personal family history.
- Think of the construct of your personal family history.
- Chronologically is relatively straightforward or do you prefer themes?
- Place photographs and images appropriately, with clear descriptions.
- Consider what you have enjoyed with others' stories and memoirs.
- Ensure you have relevant dates and places.
- Use the lists in this chapter as personal prompts.
- Avoid simply placing landmarks of life. What were your feelings? Why? How?
- Bring people and special occasions alive.
- Are there ancestors who fascinate you, whom you wish to write about?
- You could include images of, say: school reports; wedding invitations; birth, marriage and death notices; newspaper articles; ancestor letters; siblings and parents.
- Have a family tree outlined in the back of the memoir.
- Include appropriate creative writing and artwork.
- Get descriptions of yourself from other family members and friends.

- Plan attachments of labelled photographs that illustrate the memoir.
- Consider your life's historical and family history timelines for inclusion.
- Check online for final format ideas.

Ideas in this chapter could be stimulators for your children compiling their own life histories and trigger words for their 'autobiographies' could also be selected from such words as the following.

- Aunts and uncles: Who? When seen? Links with?
- Best game: Which? In school? At home? After school? Who played?
- Birthdays: Best present? How celebrated? Any special birthday? Traditions?
- Careers: What would you like to be? Why?
- Celebrations: What are the main family and personal celebrations?
- Chores: Which ones? Your feelings? When done? At what age?
- Church: Church attended? Your feelings about church?
- Christmas: Best part? Favourite present? The day? The night before?
- Cooking: Best meal you cooked? How did you learn? What to learn?
- Dad: Describe? Habits? Interaction with? Best features?
- Dating: When started? Favourite date? Who do you remember?
- Difficulties: Physical, mental, emotional? How were these handled?
- Failures: Anything memorable? Failures conquered?
- Favourites: Things, Memories, People, Games, Places, Objects, Days?
- Friends: Who? Why? Shared pleasures?
- Fright: Worst fright? False fright? Overcoming fright?
- Fun: What is fun? Personal fun? Shared fun? Family fun?
- Grandparents: Being with them? Describe them? Have you learned from them?
- Growing up: Challenging? Best things? More independent? Learned what?
- Happiness: By myself? With someone else? Happy times in my life?
- Hideout: Where? Why? Hideout in my head? Best hideout?
- Hobbies: What? Hobby changes? What appeals about a hobby?
- Holiday: Favourite? Why? Ideal holiday? Preparing, packing and returning?
- Homes: This home? My room? Good things and what could be improved?
- Jobs: Responsibility? How to learn? Good jobs? Disliked jobs?
- Leisure time: Activities? Favourite leisure time? When is leisure time?
- Life's lessons: What am I learning about life? How do I learn?

- Meals: Your role at mealtime? Likes and dislikes? Meals elsewhere?
- Memorabilia: Any special possessions? Why are they special? How kept?
- Mum: Describe? Habits? Interaction with? Best features?
- Music: Favourite? Have tastes changed? How accessed?
- Mystery: What do I wonder about? Why?
- Names: Nicknames? Like your name? What do others call you?
- Neighbours: Describe them? Interaction with?
- Occupations: Family members' occupations? Your preferred occupation?
- Overseas: Travelled overseas? Where do you wish to go when older? Why?
- Party: Best parties? Your perfect birthday party? Party setbacks?
- Pets: Describe them? Favourite choice of pet? Responsibilities?
- Places: Main places in your life? Regular weekly places?
- Play: Favourite places? Why? Playing alone? With friends?
- Playground: Activities? Skipping rhymes, tag, hopscotch and four-square?
- Pleasures: What are your personal pleasures? Why?
- Reading: Do you like reading? Why? Favourite four books? Latest reading?
- Sadness: We all feel sad times. When, and why, have been yours?
- Scared: Everyone has felt scared. When and why have you been scared?
- School: Getting there? Favourite subjects? Why? School day?
- Secrets: Did you have a secret that is no longer a secret? Secret signs?
- Shopping: Favourite shopping? Boring shopping? Shopping with whom?
- Shyness: When are you ever shy? How could you help a shy friend?
- Siblings: Characteristics? Interests? Family roles?
- Special Friends: Why are they? What do you do together? Secrets? Special times?
- Special places: Where? When? Describe two? Describe the ideal place for you?
- Sports: Participation? Watching? In your weekly life? Sport in the family?
- Success: What has been a success for you? How do you describe success?
- Surprise: Best surprises in your life so far, in and out of your family?
- Teacher: Who is, or has been, your best teacher? Why?
- Transport: Do you cycle, walk or drive? How do you get to school or work?

- Travel: Which is the best place you have travelled to? What travel goals?
- Typical days: What is a typical day in the week and at the weekend?
- Work: Describe part-time or full-time job and how you feel about it.

Extended Family Considerations

Family linkage terminology may confuse researchers. Find a simple chart or explanation that shows your uncle or aunt, a cousin, a first cousin, a first cousin-once-removed, a second cousin, a great-uncle etc. This is probably best shown with an outline of a broad family tree. Youngsters can enjoy compiling a sheet that shows these terms and real names of relations who fit. Do not get mired in the use of these terms.

1. First cousins share a grandparent.
2. Second cousins share a great-grandparent.
3. Third cousins share a great-great-grandparent.
4. Fourth cousins share a great-great-great grandparent.

It may be, as in the author's family, that third cousins and fourth cousins are motivators, fellow researchers and providers of stimuli and ancestral knowledge. Fourth cousins are usually the widest range of relatives with whom we may personally be familiar. It can be rewarding to connect with third cousins who have a knowledge of the direct family through their being in the whole family. Every family seems to have at least one branch with material in their treasure trove, sometimes without fully realising its importance.

Gather copies of birth, marriage and death certificates that you can access online or which are held by family members. Circulate these. They often generate supplementary information from parents, grandparents and family relatives.

Prepare a family newsletter, which could become the responsibility of a couple of your family members. The newsletter can provide, and seek, information. It can bring the wider family closer together. It may increasingly become a research update with findings and questions. It could include quizzes, writings and photographs. Family members might write obituaries of ancestors who have taken their interest. That will be a spur to even more complete research process.

The extended family may provide photographs or memorabilia associated with your direct family line. The family history project is a great time for sorting photographs. Adults can select these, sort them, give the setting and name people in them. There could be copies for each family member. Explore possible enhancements of these without distorting them. As noted earlier, track down the work of photograph interpreters, especially Jayne Shrimpton.

Researching the Family Homes

Why not research your home and previous family homes? Teenagers could become adept at this. Interview grandparents and friends for successive home places. Check out sites offering free information on land locations. Family history magazines have articles on researching your past home. Explore Google Earth to tour family places and then save your images. Online searches increasingly reveal information on searching a home's history. Children can be assisted to research aspects of the list below. Photographs can be found through wider family and friends' collections. Locate maps online. What were the local landmarks? Check also the British Association for Local History at **www.balh.org.uk**, Trace My House at **www.tracemyhouse.com** and Local History Online at **www.local-history.co.uk**.

Teenage researchers could contact persons living in what were their ancestors' family homes and ask if they would email a photo of the home in return for the teenager sending additional information on that home and its past occupants. To pinpoint residential addresses, consider the range of other possible sources:

- Architects
- Armed services registration and next-of-kin addresses
- Book club and social group information
- Building construction records
- Census returns
- Church membership records
- Court records of ownership, divorce, inquest, legal cases and wills
- Cultural and ethnic memberships
- Elderly local residents
- Electoral rolls
- Extreme weather or other emergency reports
- Government surveys such as Tithe Applotment, Griffiths Valuation, petitions
- Hobby or craft organisations in town that have an address for a past family member
- Insurance companies of the time
- Legal aspects such as probates, deeds and land titles
- Letter of enquiry to the local newspaper

- Letters held by family relatives
- Library subscriber lists
- Local archives records
- Local businesses, ranging from 'olden days delivery' to car sales offices
- Local club records
- Local genealogical society assistance
- Local government building approvals and correspondence
- Magazine subscribers of past years
- Mail deliveries
- Masonic lodge records
- Medical, health and local hospital records
- Memories of the home held by old friends
- Newspaper advertisements, local news mentions, notices and subscriptions
- Paper deliveries
- Petitions
- Photograph sources.
- Political party membership
- Rate payments
- Real estate and realtors living locally
- School enrolments records, registers and other school records
- Shops that may have had accounts with a name and address
- Sport club and cultural organisation addresses of members

One grandparent home which became part of family home histories.

- Trade directories
- Undertaker records
- Wills
- Workplace records

The enterprising family researcher will use search engines for finding further locational advice. Be creative and seek virtual tours of the area. Would searches of YouTube, Facebook or Pinterest yield assistance? Books on utilising county and local history records are available.

You may locate your kin in *The Gazetteer of British Place Names*, a substantial index of over 280,000 index entries. See such other internet sites as the British Library with its increasing content of places and the National Library of Ireland Digital Photographs. Utilise your search engines. *Tracing Ancestors Through County Records* by Jonathan Oates (Pen & Sword, 2016) provides an overview and is a reminder that churches and schools associated with the family's past may still be standing. At least, check about ancestors in their once local library, local newspapers, civic records or workplaces.

The keen researcher can now be challenged to see if they can locate family locations and homes recorded in early surveys, as far back as *Tithe Applotment Books* and *Griffiths Valuations* in Ireland and the *Hearth Tax* ('Chimney Tax') in Scotland. Search engines are the key.

It is inevitable that some of your family moved overseas, migrated or served in the military or had no choice of destination as they were convicts. Youngsters will enjoy tracking them down, especially the last of these, and checking migration and passenger lists on major sites. They will have approximate years from census information and newspaper reports in their homeland and new land. As with all ancestral individual research, check out names on free sites such as FamilySearch, then head to the library's free access to Ancestry. The use of world maps and generational display forms, given out at the scene-setting family gathering, now come into their own.

Family Myths, Stories and Names

Every family has stories or 'myths' from the past. 'Great-great-grandmother was a suffragette.' 'About two hundred years ago one of our ancestors was a pirate.' 'Your name comes from a Welsh ancestor of the 1700s.' One granddaughter carries Garonne as her second name. Where did this come from? Family legend says her direct ancestor, James Bennett, whose wife was pregnant when he left on a business-orientated voyage to England from Australia, was shipwrecked and the *Garonne* was the boat that rescued him. Hence, his return to Australia, with heartfelt emotions of relief, was said to lead to his first-born child being named Hilda Garonne Bennett. Various family members have chased the story to check the veracity of this family legend. They eventually tracked passenger lists and searched historical newspapers. These led to the discovery of James Bennett having been a passenger on the *Garonne* when it hit the African coast in 1878. Miraculously the badly damaged boat eventually got back into the ocean and managed to safely steam home to England. Bennett and his wife, Charlotte (née Hyland) thankfully named their baby daughter, Garonne. The name has been given to daughters in the family through some 144 subsequent years. This account reflects the need for researchers to record the full names of family members and ancestors and to explore their family stories and possible myths.

Where did our family names come from? What are their meanings? Do they link with the historical timeline we maintain alongside our direct family line? How can we check these? Often, first names were given because of a name borne by a prominent person of the time. Some ancestors may have been given a name that underscores the continuity of successive generations. As a boy, the author was intrigued by having Charles as a given name after preceding generations of Charles. Consider checking the Guild of One-Name Studies and sites with articles on names, their origins and name changes.

Are there any extant family traditions? Can older family members recount any of these? Are there traditions related to births, birthdays, Christmas and special occasions, marriages, deaths, national days, Halloween or Guy Fawkes, graduations, Memorial Day, Anzac Day, Armistice Day / VE Day, planting a new tree, a new home, special gifts, national holidays, welcomes, farewells, meals, passing on family history, anniversaries and achievements?

You will have budgeted for finances for the planned research. Be careful with costs. Critically consider the costs of accessing online material and any software that needs to be upgraded. Check search engine entries such as **www.genealogy-software-review.topten** to locate recommendations to be considered for appropriate software.

Do not rush into paid site membership, which may be costly and not necessarily yield lodes of gold-seam family information. Some free sites have been noted previously. Often, they provide information which could have been costly on paid sites. It is to this field of non-cost sites and human resources we now turn.

Chapter 5

FREE SOURCES FOR YOUR FAMILY RESEARCH

Drawing from the Wider Family

Your immediate in-family sources were free, when parents and grandparents were the starting sources for first acquiring free information. Build up a list of potential interviewees from family persons, cousins of parents, close friends of parents and grandparents. Explain your family venture and offer to provide results information.

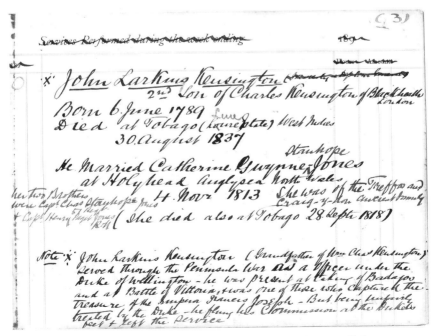

Extract from notebook of William Charles Kensington noting his grandfather.

Revisit interview questions in Chapter 4. There may be members of the extended family who have information, photographs or memorabilia linked to aspects of those questions and your direct ancestors. Do any of them have a family tree you may copy?

The wider you cast the family research net, to second, third and even fourth cousins, the more likely is the chance of gaining direct ancestor knowledge that is new to you. These wider family linkages could be consolidated with a shared blog, family newsletters, social media, additions to online family trees, sharing photographs and stories of memorabilia portraits and photographs of family persons. The author's wider family have contributed items to each other, with copies of letters, nineteenth-century diary entries, copies of certificates and school records, photographs of miniatures from the eighteenth century, cassette tapes of interviews placed on the computer, DVDs copied from 'old-time' silent movies of family occasions, present-day support and books with dates and copperplate inscriptions.

Online Research Can Be Free

An enormous amount of material is obtained through search engines. Having gathered vital information from family and friends you can search possible sites widely. Youngsters are probably skilled in Googling and searching with key words but may need assistance to select other search engines and the most appropriate key words to use in a search. They could be introduced to other search engines such as HotBot, Yahoo, Yandex, Ask, Altavista, Baidu and Bing. You may wish to check on whether you have complete privacy with a particular search engine. A Google search of 'The best search engine sites' is revealing in its findings, as is search engine journeying for 'free genealogy or family history sites'. Now that young family members are moving into online research, compile a limited prioritised list of family history words and search terms and give them to family members to assist their research.

Parents who have become familiar with free sites in the early stage of developing basic research practices should impart the need to research these for specific information before accessing paid sites. The free sites give younger researchers more opportunity for framing research questions, learning further research skills and the relief of cost-free errors. There are many helpful free family history sites, found through search engines, browsing family tree magazines, checking the well-recommended books noted in Chapter 2 and checking web sites noted in Appendix 1. Do check the OGI (Online Genealogical Index) site, especially if researching United Kingdom sources.

Books and Magazines

For those with Irish or possible Irish ancestry, check Chris Paton's *Tracing Your Irish Family History on the Internet* (Pen and Sword, 2nd edition 2019) and *Tracing Your Irish Ancestors Through Land Records* (Pen and Sword 2021) You have Scottish ancestry? Then obtain Paton's book *Tracing Your Scottish Family History on the Internet* (Pen and Sword, 2020). Pen and Sword's specialised Family History division should be checked for books with particular strengths for English counties research.

Unlock the Past (Gould) has a growing list of helpful but reasonably priced books such as Smith (2016) and Hicks (2016). This site is worthy of consideration, particularly by parents planning this whole-family research adventure and thinking of a controlled budget.

Family history magazines can be excellent. Check them, as one is more USA orientated but has outstanding research articles which can often be downloaded free, and the other two are more UK orientated but with research that is not limited to the UK. The three most highly recommended, personally, are available online and in bookshops.

- *Family Tree*   **www.family-tree.co.uk**
- *Family Tree Magazine*   **www.familytreemagazine.com**
- *Who Do You Think You Are?*   **www.whodoyouthinkyouaremagazine**

Others to explore are: *Your Genealogy Today; Internet Genealogy; Your Family History; National Genealogical Society Quarterly; Family History Monthly; Discover Your Ancestors* and regular publications by genealogical organisations.

The biggest free site, that has worldwide recognition for its free records, is FamilySearch. This site was started by the Latter Day Saints (LDS) Church and has grown to contain millions of vital records and is strong in its Great Britain content. The researcher should have a clear goal, heading for Search-Records, to determine what is available. It will help your family researcher, if unfamiliar with FamilySearch, to go to the guidance of **familysearch.org/ask/gettingstarted** to read about this vast site of potential riches. The related site of the FamilySearch research wiki is a helpful site to explore as it guides the researcher into a wider range of sources. Family members may wish to check out information at the physical location of their nearest FamilySearch centre. Check the FamilySearch site for locating your nearest centre.

Utilising Primary Research Sites

Major sites usually have some free guides that assist the researcher to utilise available records or provide relevant free guides to research. The unsuspecting researcher needs to ensure that they are not drawn into 'free access' that turns, after a certain time, into paid access. Some sites automatically renew your annual subscription which highlights the need for the researcher to maintain a clear list of their subscription sites, payments and dates of renewal or discontinuation. The key subscription sites of Ancestry, Findmypast, MyHeritage and TheGenealogist often have some databases available at no cost, offer free trials of their site or provide short-term free access. You can open a free Ancestry account as a Registered Guest Account. This can stay operative as you will not be charged. It is limited but could be explored for lodging your family tree and receiving responses to this, searching free Ancestry databases, posting to Ancestry Message boards, accessing Ancestry Blog and other opportunities.

Your local library will probably have access for its patrons to use the full Ancestry subscription site at no cost. In certain circumstances, many archives and libraries offer their online subscription facilities at no cost.

The family could utilise the MyHeritage site. The site informs, as others do, on how to construct a family tree that will be online for others to see. Use this site to automatically find matches in historical records, family trees and photos. Advanced researchers can take advantage of family history tools from MyHeritage such as Family Tree Builder software. They will enjoy learning photograph enhancement such as MyHeritage In Color and MyHeritage Photo Enhancer.

Particular sites become particular favourites. Many researchers have a pleasant surprise when discovering Cyndi's List or drawing upon WikiTree, which reportedly has some thirteen million persons of earlier generations. Examples of what can be found are also seen on ancestry.com and the RootsWeb site.

Free Basic Data Records

There is a list of free family history sites in Appendix 1. The family could divide these up and work on locating site information and site research results. Check out **freeukgenealogy.org.uk** as it has three websites of free material on census, births, marriages, deaths and registers records. If one of the family is seeking a free source of England or Wales births, marriages and deaths then lead them to **freebmd.org.uk**. They can then try freeReg. Youngsters can utilise **freereg.org.uk** to seek transcriptions of parish records from England, Wales and Scotland. The free sites offer research opportunities for youngsters at no charge and invariably bring discoveries that excite them which may be followed up, if necessary, on paid sites. If faced with a 'brickwall' in their research, serious researchers would possibly check the (not free) Joiner Marriage Index with its charges for marriage records in England and Wales before 1837.

Explain electoral rolls and census returns to family researchers as needed. Before utilising census searches on paid genealogical sites your young researchers can check out **freecen.org.uk** for United Kingdom census returns. Undertaking this relatively straightforward search usually yields ancestors and their families, birth dates and places, addresses and occupations.

Tracking a person through census returns every ten years from 1841 will indicate their movements and, possibly, lead to knowledge of the years in which a death or immigration occurred between census returns. The census-listed age and birth location of family persons will lead to knowledge of where to seek actual birth information. The accompanying use of a map by the family researcher can build up sequential family

Extract from Broneifion part of Llanystumdwy census.

movements. Your family will enjoy linking census returns with that map and the use of Google Earth to obtain more understanding. Census returns often have the names of the direct ancestor's siblings, which can be recorded by the researcher to use at a later date, in working around a seeming deadlock.

In Ireland, England, Wales and Scotland the National Archives and the National Library sources have engaging fields for any researcher. Do not rush this initially but gain a broad understanding of their research riches. Get their research guides and subscribe to their free and often informative newsletters. Try, for example, the National Archives of England at **nationalarchives.gov.uk.** At least, they have helpful notes on genealogical research and their archival records; at best, they may reveal new information on your ancestor when found after following through one of their sixty-five online research guides.

The National Archives of Ireland and the National Library of Ireland are often rewarding for some listings from census records, Tithe Applotment Books (1823–1837) and the Calendars of Wills and Administrations (1858–1922). The National Library of Ireland is now a good source for Catholic Church records.

The National Library of Wales (NLW) has been significant for young researchers. The roots and generations of the Jones and Anwyl trees of the author's family, in Anglesey and Caernarvonshire especially, came to life in the Welsh resources. Try the Discover menu and the NLW Resources divisions as possible sources. It is a boon for family members to find wills in the NLW. While researching online in Wales, hunt up Member Societies of the Association of Family History Societies of Wales sites as they lead to the county society you may wish to explore.

In the British Isles and Ireland, the initial starting site yielding access to diverse national records may well be **irishgenealogy.ie;** the National Archives of Ireland also should be searched at **genealogy. nationalarchives.ie** as this latter source has census returns, wills, and tithe records. In Scotland, try searching **scotlandspeople.gov.uk** (the search is basic and does require payment of a fee to view documents) and National Records of Scotland at **nrscotland.gov.uk/research/guides/ birth-death-and-marriage-records/statutory-registers-of-births-deaths- and-marriages** with its comprehensive access to these core legal records.

Free Print Sources

Historical newspapers are great, being rarely searched fully without some discoveries. There are many retrieval newspaper sites around the world. If you have ancestors who migrated to Australia, or New Zealand, then draw upon 'trove' for Australian newspapers and Papers Past for New Zealand newspaper searches. For Canada, see the Canada Newspaper Archives. These can dovetail with migrant shipping and passenger lists. The USA yields Chronicling America and rich sources found when using search words such as USA historical newspapers. Again, take any 'free offer' carefully. The British Newspaper Archive has wide resources of articles from United Kingdom and Ireland newspapers. This can be augmented with accessing *The Gazette* – the government's official paper with entries ranging from military appointments to bankruptcies, from government department appointments to naturalisations.

Books, informal biographies and informally published local histories may be found in second-hand bookshops, rare book suppliers and libraries near your family's earlier residential areas. There is an ever-growing yield of family histories. In *On Record*, written in 1922 by Isaac Coates, the author's great-grandfather, we learn of local North Yorkshire customs and traditions of the early nineteenth century and family stories such as the cauldron of gold guineas discovered by his dry-waller grandfather in 1779. He describes his home village of Gayles, 6 miles north-west of Richmond, in the 1840s and the local district in some depth. How else would we have learned so readily of rural life of the times, the Fenwicks, Parlours and Dinsdales?

Family memorabilia are another stimulus for free family information. One particular example illustrates strongly the value of contact and interaction with members of the wider family. A cousin of the author's mother, who married later in life and had no children, died. Original miniature portraits that had been in my great-grandfather's possession now became my inheritance from my mother's cousin. The subjects of the miniatures were Charles Kensington (1749–1807), my great-great-great-great-grandfather, and Pierre de la Porte (1710–1804). This stimulated research on the De la Portes as Huguenots and led to certain geographic and genealogical research in France. It also led to research on the miniaturist painter, G.D. Engleheart. Every family has

Pierre de la Porte (1737–1804), father of Louisa de la Porte (1754–1841).

the similar possibility of learning more of their direct family ancestors through actions of their wider family members. Such relatives may have memorabilia that leads you to greater knowledge of an ancestor or, at least, the stimulation of researching a particular ancestor.

One lasting free source is that of fiction. This may seem unusual but authentic writers of historical novels, for example, present the reader with a valid setting of times and places. Consider *Sharpe's Fortress* by Bernard Cornwell (Harper Collins, 1998). This has a focus upon the Gawilghur battle in 1803. The book is a well-researched, albeit fictional, portrayal of this battle. It features, in part of the story, the author's four times great-grandfather, Lieutenant Colonel William Kenny.

Parents may have cleared the way for young ones to access paid sites, which could now be targeted. After their systematic exploration of free sites, the young family researchers will feel reasonably confident in their skills to move into research more independently, which will yield intrinsic rewards of achievement for children as family historians.

Chapter 6

CHILDREN AS FAMILY HISTORIANS

Family History from the Past to the Present for the Future

The whole family is engaged in this research adventure. Consider each family member carefully. You are preparing young people to be able researchers and users of social media and research sites. You are leading them into future family history leadership roles through enjoyable, stimulating and rewarding research. How do you best bring each youngster into the research adventure domain? Some may be happy to research an individual whom you suggest is worth finding out about, while others may prefer following their own field of interest that links with family history. If the latter, then think of their technical skills, internet abilities and interests. Follow up on earlier suggestions about young family members' wishes to research particular interests. How will that particular interest be linked with a family person, era or timeline?

Sophia could easily draw up a large chart showing a fashion timeline and a family timeline. Then she can develop links. Her starting point would be herself – with diary extracts, an account of the clothes she has to wear, such as school uniform or for Guides, and of her choices of clothes. Do parents, grandparents and others have information on clothes worn in different generations? What are the more significant aspects of the photographs that young family members should look for? Consider clothing for work, leisure, special occasions, armed services, and formal settings. Will you find any family person in uniform to show the family? Do wedding dresses change over time? One young researcher found Cyndi's List had extensive female ancestor material. She might begin a fashion scrapbook, files of written and visual material, photographs and newspaper and magazine articles. Perhaps she would interview peers, parents, grandparents and family friends about their clothes interests

Ethel Alberta Kensington (née Coates) 1878–1932, on the left.

Norma Bessie Kensington, daughter of Norman Charles Kensington and Ethel.

and fashions of the times, formal and informal. Sophia would search for information with questions such as 'What did our female ancestors wear?' Sophia could borrow books from the library which then assist her in filling out her fashion history timeline in parallel with her family history timeline. What are her family predecessors wearing in photos through time?

Will she consider male fashions, or will her focus stay on female fashions? Would she interview a fashion reporter and seek advice on her research? Will she include sport fashions, such as swimwear, athletes' gear or tennis players' fashions? Can anyone help her learn from theses or college research and writings on fashion change? Have cheerleaders changed through the decades? Which ex-sport participant women in her mother's and grandmother's generations might engage in interviews? Which dressmakers and couturiers would she speak with? Who can inform her on everyday wear, work clothes, formal clothing and social dress through the past 200 years? Sophia could then seek any existing family records such as historical newspaper reports which often comment upon what the bride and attendants were wearing at weddings or women wore on certain social occasions. What influenced fashion in her family over time? Interviews with fashion history researchers could be followed up.

Sophia's search engines quickly locate 'fashion history' and 'learning about fashion history' sites which draw immediate interest. See the site Sophia would find at **https://fashionhistory.fitnyc.edu** for example. Then she sets her photographs out and considers Jayne Shrimpton's information on interpreting fashion and photographs, especially Shrimpton's *Fashion and Family History*, (Pen & Sword, 2020).

Sophia, being bilingual, might then wish to research her female French ancestors' fashions or, possibly more prosaically, locate immigrant ship lists of clothes. This illustrates the diverse ways a youngster in the family can carry out research on a particular area of interest and further illustrates our guiding definition that *family history is a history of the direct family in the past and in the present – recorded for the future*.

Imagine a young girl or boy finding the family's successive church linkages or arts expression or participation in a civic or cultural field through newspaper archives which mention an ancestor in a past local newspaper. Newspaper archives offer the chance to search newspapers of a particular place and time. This raises the idea of young ones responding to the creative aspect of being detectives who have cases to solve. It may be this detective self-concept that draws them into the family venture.

Some youngsters have an interest in family members of the armed forces. Others may have a particular interest in gardening or books of the day or special day customs or the sea. Build up a timeline with them e.g. books on sea voyages of pioneer days. Look at grandparents' explanations of special days and build back from there. Jointly set goals and help the young ones understand initial sources of likely information they can log into. Genealogical and history magazines have excellent articles on researching in special fields of interest. Check them out and monitor their websites. Search the internet for certain historical periods and maintain the timelines you construct with your youngster.

Maya enjoyed playing the harp, composing and was in a major choir. Cleo has pleasure playing the piano and dancing. Ask them to describe the appeal of these and of their music or movement. These present-day activities will become part of the present family's record for the future family to read about and, probably, have a young family member in that generation who will relate to the insightful accounts of life from today.

Writing and Recording Today for Tomorrow

Critical entrées into the world of contemporary family history await young family members. Imagine if they could read accounts of, say, *their* great-grandparents' daily lives; reading about school, seeing drawings and artworks of their homes, going through an account of the Spanish

Flu and reading diary extracts would invariably engage youngsters' interests. Imagine your young family members writing, for future family members, their account of the Covid-19 period. Present-day youngsters can construct their own collections of material illustrating their present-day life and then work out how to hand this on to future generations. This will be enhanced through parent and grandparent interest and support.

Making a basketball hoop for a son or daughter is little different from making a piece of clothing or a toy for one of them. Each could be part of a story or the tracing of a family thread. Even the youngest children can contribute tellingly to a family history time capsule (see Chapter 9). In effect, the suggestion is that, with parental guidance, each child could compile their own personal life portfolio and pass this on. Your children as young as 4 years or 5 years could be interviewed and the results placed with the other family member portrayals of their present-day lives.

Family history places an emphasis upon recording the present for the future. Children, as family historians, can undertake informative, challenging and enjoyable 'in the present' accomplishments such as:

- An account of the week at school
- An account of a parent's week
- An account of a sibling's week
- An account of their 'spare time' activities
- An autobiography, with pictures and photographs
- Art, craft and wall hanging illustrations of family life
- Attractive folders of named and dated photographs
- Church involvement
- Copies of school reports and awards
- Diaries of a typical week or special holiday
- Drawings by youngest family members to be put in the time capsule
- Family occasions
- Favourite poetry and stories – some of which they may have written
- Home life, chores and routines, personal time
- Information from Birth, Marriage and Death (BMD) records
- Interviews with family members, including siblings, parents, grandparents, aunts and uncles
- Interviews of the youngster by their sibling
- Notes on their own community involvement e.g. clubs, Scouts, teams, voluntary work, tree planting
- Paintings or drawings they create as visual records of their childhood.
- Personal records such as school, sport or cultural recognition
- Personal timelines for each family member

- Pets in the family lives. Interview your pet?
- Photographs with labels
- Sport, hobbies, cultural or interest group activities
- Stories of siblings' activities
- Typical school or weekend days
- Writing and illustrating a record of holidays
- Writing letters to their future selves

A holiday with the author's children and their fourth cousins had a diary of daily activities and what they learned that day about their family. The diary includes drawings and annotations by the four under 12-year-olds. Some drew themselves or ancestors or family members or family heirlooms and put descriptions and dates with them.

What would your youngsters wish to know, today, about the young lives of their ancestors? What would future family members like to know about your young ones' present family lives? Children can assemble contemporary photographs and write about them, especially of memorably different days.

Their older siblings can help. Using photographs gives greater personal meaning to family descendants and can be enhanced and placed on a family tree. There are many photograph-enhancing aids online, some of which are free. Some bring greater clarity to somewhat indistinct photos and others can colour them in a skilful way. Check out MyHeritage for examples of how to enhance your photographs with photo enhancement, photo restoration and photo coloration.

Every family has past and present stories! Some families may like to use art or writing or craft to illustrate their past family history, their present family history or one selected person in it. In the author's family are the 'Gavin Stories', and 'John Stories', which are pages and pages of specific childhood farm life memories of these two brothers, compiled by their brother and sister half a century after they occurred, as living gifts for a dying brother and the other who became terminally ill. Some of the story titles were:

Maya and Cleo skiing as a favoured sport.

- Chores
- Earning pocket money
- Eeling in the farm creek
- Family members
- Family rules and punishments
- Farm animals and pets
- Football in winter
- Games we played – inside and outside
- Gardening and grounds chores
- Horse riding
- Milking the cows
- The naughty brother(s)
- Once Upon a Christmas Time.
- On the house roof
- Our tree huts and hideaways
- Pranks
- School
- School Bus
- Smuggling cookies
- Sport in our lives
- Sunday School and church
- Swimming in the creek

Mum and dad had taken you and Jayne to town for Christmas shopping. Gav and I headed for the parental boudoir and opened up their cupboard, albeit a trifle nervously. There was a big parcel there from Aunty Gwen and Uncle Norm. We wanted to see what presents we were getting! We quickly, and oh-so-carefully, opened the parcel. Then we saw the little cards with our names on, stuck on wrapped-up presents. As carefully as we used to take your fudge when you weren't looking, we opened up Gav's present and mine. Gav's face fell because he was getting underwear! Then we opened your present and you, the lucky nephew, were getting a toy car. The brains of brothers operate in mysterious and parallel lines...Gav and I looked at each other with one thought...why don't we swap the cards for Gav and John's presents???? We wrapped up the parcels and put your name card on what was originally Gavin's present and put Gav's name card on what was originally your present.

Christmas Day arrived. We always had the same routine of church and then presents from around the tree. It came time for opening the presents from Aunty Gwen and Uncle Norm. I opened mine. Then Gav opened his. Gav was ecstatic to open his and find a mighty good toy car! Then you opened yours. What a forlorn figure was our youngest brother, who stood in front of us all saying, "All I got was this underwear." You held them both against yourself and added, dolefully, "And they're too big for me anyway!"

A 'Brother John' story which all the grandchildren now tell.

These are being assembled into more lasting formats for future generations, giving insights into the lives and times of those who will then be their forebears. Check sites that may help you with such stories.

One grandparent has an agreement with her primary school (elementary school) grandchildren that if they can recite ten generations of a direct family line they then get a pleasing financial reward – if they can add births, marriages and deaths that reward markedly increases! A 10-year-old granddaughter quickly mastered this task! Now, there's an early genealogist – or entrepreneurial accountant!

Older children can help younger siblings master opportunities to check overseas resource bases for immigration, passenger lists and archival records.

Names

Young family members can research names. Have names been passed down through generations? Have they changed? If so, are we aware of this as we research? Consider names beginning with O' or Mac and those dropped or reset after some time. What about similar sounding names, perhaps misspelled on official forms? Do we consider Storie when researching Story? Do our names have meanings? Do they have special family meanings? Does Bodhi have a special meaning? How and when did these names start? What alternative spellings do we find? Henry Waite, the son of Richard Wayet and Harriet Huthwaite, was often known by the surname White. It may be that a past surname became a second name and that leads into a new exploration of its importance and relevance in the family's story. Libraries often have surname books. Children like exploring True or False meanings of names, as in: Smith (to strike hard with metal, as with a blacksmith?); Johnson (a son of John?); Hobday (Hobb the servant? Servant of Hobb?); Cornes (associated with corn?); Mollie (a pet form of Mary?); Lorraine (of Lorraine in France?); Joel (a biblical name?); Archibald (a no-hair archer?) or Kerry (from County Kerry?). A young family member could do this with chosen family names and they could also see the Guild of One-Name Studies at **www.one-name.org**.

Cross-generation Commonalities

Youngsters enjoy linking an ancestor with a historical happening.

A young family member noted, on Christmas Day, that an ancestor, Charles Jephson William Kensington, died in distant New Zealand on Christmas Day, 1877, far from his birthplace of Le Havre, France, his marriage in Criccieth, Wales, and his home in Worton, Wiltshire. His family biography would lead to a world map and history timelines.

The author decided New Zealand family places should be seen. Visiting the rather isolated Port Charles area, his children were photographed one winter, with the fallen tombstone – desolate evidence of their ancestor. To die in Port Charles of apoplexy on Christmas Day was not the desired end for a Westminster education, which saw him listed in the Old Boys' Register as 'married and gone to New Zealand', to which he sailed in 1862 with Olivia Maturin and their ten children. My two children, that day in remote Port Charles, knew the oaks on the family estate in Wiltshire were three centuries old, but Kensington's own pyre burned slowly through his two chilled descendants standing above his bones under a lone macrocarpa on that distant land. Of such, is the tracing of your family history with the whole family. We all can find our parallels.

Charles Jephson William Kensington who died at Port Charles, Coromandel, New Zealand.

Samples of timeline searches could be to locate ancestor lives or dated events at the time of:

- A major national disaster
- An ancestor's birth, marriage, death or special life accomplishment
- A new government or Royal Family change through death or abdication
- Creation of an autonomous country
- Declaration of war
- Great sporting occasions
- The Holocaust
- Literature of lasting significance
- The *Mayflower*
- Pandemic lockdown
- President John Kennedy's assassination
- Royal death
- The Civil War
- The first moon landing
- The Napoleonic Wars
- The significant creation of a piece of art, music or literature

- Special occasions in a special field of interest
- Suffragette petition
- Voting rights for indigenous peoples, African Americans, women, all citizens

```
                                    IOR  L/AG/34/29/36
                                         Commissary


EXHIBIT A to which the annexed Affidavit of
S.B. this day refers dated 21st Octr.1824
                        AB

                DACCA, 17th September 1824

I RICHARD AUGUSTUS CLAYE WATSON being of sound mind
but about to proceed to the Wars where life is
uncertain have resolved to make this my last Will
and Testament

1st Being a Subscriber to the Widows Fund as Lt.
Colonel I consider that a handsome provision for
my Wife but as a last token of my regard leave
her a Miniature of my daughter Mary.

2ndly I leave whatever property I may have either
in this Country or Europe after the Sale of my
Effects and the realization of my two shares in
the Calcutta Laudable Society to my three children
MARY WATSON, WILLIAM CLAYE WATSON and DIXIE WATSON
now residing with their grandmother and aunts at
Southwell, Nottinghamshire.


3rdly I leave to my sister Mrs ROSS a miniature
picture of my daughter Mary.

AND LASTLY I request as a particular favour that
my Friends Lt.Col (Heathwaite?) Major Wm. Watson
Captain H. Ross, (T.B. Swinhoe) and Lt McIntosh
will act as Executors to this my last Will and to
the last I leave the sale of my Property in such
way as I have requested  h m, but above all I
request that no one but him may be allowed to open
my papers, he will destroy such as he may deem
proper and seal up and preserve such as may appear
likely to become useful.

Earnestly Recommending my Children to the Care and
protection of all my friends and relations I
herewith          my name and Seal in presence
of Witnesses in testimony of the validity of
this Will.
                        R.A.C. WATSON
                        Lt.Col. 44 Regt.
Witnesses
John James Paterson
    Surgeon 44 Reft  N.I.
H. (-) Mackintosh Lieut.44th Regt N.I.
```

Will of Richard Augustus Claye Watson, Lieutenant Colonel 44 Regiment. Died Dacca 1824.

- Wars, battles or declarations of peace.
- When 9/11 occurred
- When a military or political milestone occurred
- When certain music genre, folk music, jazz, rock and roll hit the music scene
- When the Spanish Flu or Covid-19 pandemic hit their country or locality

Which ancestor was involved with the occasion? What could have been their impressions and experience? This brings history *and* your family together. One aspect of family history now emerges that intrigues some family researchers. On a large diary, one 10-year-old researcher worked with a family adult to note significant family dates such as births, marriages, deaths, military engagements, specific achievements, granting of awards, anniversaries, migration dates etc. Working with her template, she noted, for those special family days, any significant historical happening and, particularly, any family member linked to that historical day. Books of days are plentiful for checking. Consider personal days linking with past events.

- 13 January is Toby's birthday. He shares the same birthday as Michael Bond, who wrote the *Paddington Bear* stories and Hugh Lofting who wrote *Dr Dolittle*.

Toby McConnell, grandson.   *Cleo Zipfel, granddaughter.*

- 22 February is Kit's birthday. George Washington was born 1732. A prominent day for Kit, a history buff, who is knowledgeable of the Washington era.
- 28 February was Kit and Anne Louise's wedding. On that day, in 1515, Teresa of Avila, the Spanish founder of the reformed Carmelites was born. In 1970 she was the first woman to be honoured as a 'Doctor of the Church'.
- 1 April is Cleo's birthday. Rachmaninov was born on that day in 1873. Parents can find a piece by Rachmaninov for Cleo, the piano player, to play.
- 17 July is Penny's birthday. It would be engaging to provide the names of people and places related to this day and for Penny and her family to have that list and the challenge to link an interest choice with one of them. Can Penny find the relevance of that day to an ancestor? A relatively easy answer is to determine which family members, with a jazz interest, were alive in 1959 when Billie Holiday died on this day.
- 8 November is Penny and Holger's wedding anniversary. Edmund Halley was born in 1656. Children enjoy reading accounts of Halley's Comet and can interview a family member who saw the comet. Today's children will hopefully see it in 2061 and can read an earlier family member account.

- 23 November is Sophia's birthday. This is the day of President John Kennedy's assassination in 1963. Sophia's grandfather wrote a poem as his diary for the day when he visited Dallas exactly twenty-five years later. Two questions that remain with Sophia's grandfather are 'Where were you when President Kennedy was killed? How did you hear about it?'

Sophia McConnell, granddaughter.

Outside a Dallas Book Depository 23.11.1988

> Parking a block away
> the book depository swung
> over us, an ominous shrike
> wing suspended in shadow,
> the secretive knoll today
> submissive under the weight
> of oxfords, questing slingbacks
> and cowboy boots.
> Before me, the mother from
> Arkansas wept for forfeiture
> of time, her words flailing
> sails in a truculent wind,
> each disconnected phrase falling
> at her daughter's scuffing feet
> as she heard anew, this very day, the
> 25th echo of the black trajectory.

- 16 December is Maya's birthday. This is when Wilhelm Grimm died in 1859. Maya grew up with a knowledge of The Brothers Grimm with their stories of Tom Thumb, Rumpelstiltskin and The Twelve Dancing Princesses.

Consider examples of historical events linked to special days or interests. Questions relating to history still resound for older generations e.g. 'Where were you at the time of 9/11?' 'Where were you at the time of the moon landing?' Consider how such days can lead to entries on the family history timeline *and* the historical timeline. In generations to come, future family members will relish hearing today's family members interviewed on 'Where were you when …?'

Maya Zipfel, granddaughter.

Chapter 7

AGILE-MINDED TEENS ARE AGILE-MINDED RESEARCHERS

This chapter provides research directions for your teenagers or independently able younger members of the family. The computer-skilled teenager will add depth to the family's research results. A skilled teenager or young adult family member could use their family's verified findings to develop a family website. Do not get your priorities awry. Research shows that family history and teenage identity and well-being make a clear difference between teenagers who engage in their narrative and those who do not. The widely noted researchers emphasise that knowing their 'familial past' is the key. (See Fivush, Duke and Bohanek, 2010).

Assist your teenagers to work from the present to the past. Obtain information from certificates. You, as a parent who initially explored basic records before the first family research gathering, will be able to provide your teenager with copies of these. Locating them in-family will save time on research the teenager might have duplicated. Order birth, marriage and death certificates if data are not found in this way or located in a past newspaper, but do check key sites and, especially, FamilySearch and those noted in Appendix 1.

Teenagers as Family Researchers

Teens will quickly become adept with sites. They will enjoy new emphases in social media which bring them face-to-face with genealogical sources and opinions on Facebook and YouTube, for example. Facebook has genealogical groups, can help locate relatives in the present and reveal unexpected information. So might the genealogical elements of such sites as Geni, Pinterest, and Rootstech (Treelines).

Given their thorough grounding and the generation of excitement in planning, your teenagers can readily dig into Ancestry and Findmypast sites, if costs of this are agreed upon within the family or if the teenager accesses a site through the local library. We want them to become familiar with FamilySearch and MyHeritage. One teenager has discovered Success for Genealogy which leads to rich sources at Google sites such as Google News Archive and Google Books. The Foundation for On-Line Genealogy has WeRelate which is worthy of a quick check.

Teenagers can add to the historical and family timelines. They can compile a map of their country, locating family places and placing ancestors with their tree number. Locations could include home and work addresses, university and school settings and workplaces. A further project could be that of exploring the history of homes lived in.

Teens can compile a world map of family locations. They can locate passenger lists, census returns and military records of ancestors. Newspaper searches may yield migrant information. Map locations could be numbered for the ancestors now associated with locations.

The roles of older children can range widely. Some will become engrossed in their own research, some will share and some may feel negative about their lack of skills or research results. Older children can aid and guide sibling research. Some families foster pairing of the researchers. Is there a local history source? Was the selected ancestor in local politics, a guild or union, the church or public service? Were they involved with any organisation? Are there local newspaper reports?

Seeking Gayles, North Yorkshire, site of the Coates farm.

Teenagers Locating Past Publications

Finding publications and books from the past can bring unexpected rewards. The capable teenager's research can be augmented with a search for digitised books at sites such as **familysearch.org/library/books**. Have your teenager explore the Internet Archive.

Teenager's Military Research

The Internet Archive yielded information on the Seventy-Third Regiment (73rd Rgt). The *London Gazette* and The Army Lists were checked. The next source tried was Fowler (Pen and Sword, 2007) with its 'Top Ten Military Sites'. Army lists noted William Crowe Kenny of the 73rd Rgt. The young researcher then traced the military father of William Crowe Kenny to Gawilghur and the military son to New Zealand. Marriages were found and new families marked onto the family and historical timelines ... and so it goes.

Research Skills Finesse

Does your teenager know the subtle skills of research? It will be advantageous to employ specific search skills which limit search questions to what they specifically seek. A ready example is the use of parentheses or quotation marks to assist search wording, leading speedily to good results. There may be a family member, tertiary student, workmate or friend skilled in research techniques. Typing in the name of an ancestor, James Story, may produce a plethora of results with the two words appearing separately somewhere but not provide information on the specific person. To focus this search upon James Story we could use (James Story) or 'James Story'. All family members will gain from simple instructions to help their searching. Books on research skills will be in your library. Information on techniques is found in search engine results. Understanding the finer techniques means information is found more quickly and more specifically. This skill acquisition can motivate and sustain teenager interests in researching.

Your teenagers are intelligent and imaginative. In the search for family homes it was Aaron who decided to contact volunteer fire brigade bases to obtain his direct ancestor's details and home address. Dionne outdid this when she researched direct family line cemeteries. One grave had flowers on it at the anniversary of the ancestor's death. It also seemed well-maintained. How did she carry out her research? Consider information from the cemetery, contact with local florists, leaving a note on the grave, checking a range of family names in the electoral roll, checking nearby graves, reading the obituary notice in the local newspaper at the time of the ancestor's passing, communicating with the undertakers, writing to the local newspaper and checking with grandparents. Now, if a teenager is so dogged and creative in thought, we are reminded of the research challenges that our family members can solve.

Teenager Writing

Examples of published teenager writing are plentiful, often as a result from adult encouragement. Consider the subjects they could write about for special interest publications, magazines, newspapers and reputable online outlets. Special days in the year can evoke a related family history article. Decide which magazine or publication will be contacted about submitting a possible article. If the teenager has a special interest they researched, then contact an appropriately themed magazine. Perhaps the teen offers, or includes, a brief overview of their proposed article. Help the youngster with this enquiry. This may well stimulate them to have their work published. This all helps their family history interests but, especially, fosters more self-confidence in the youngster, gives them a new field of expression and an enhanced belief in their abilities. Topics come to mind.

1. A fictitious but factually accurate interview with an ancestor.
2. A remarkable family member.
3. An account of a predecessor's life in terms of her struggle for equality.
4. An account of a predecessor's life in terms of their achievements.
5. An account of a predecessor's life in terms of their military career.
6. An outline of how family research is done.
7. Carpentry tools of yesteryear.
8. Cemetery dates and inscriptions.

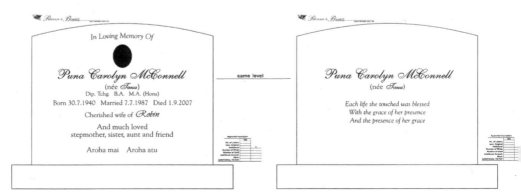

Cemetery headstone of an incomparable woman. The front was formal, the rear was essential truth. The inscriptions speak to all later generations.

9. Christmas Day for one hundred family years.
10. Church life in a family's history.
11. Family fashions in one family for a century.
12. Family history research and its unexpected rewards.
13. Farming changes over 150 family years.
14. Fashion through the ages.
15. Fifty years of family cars and trucks.
16. How our garden changed over 100 years.
17. How to start a family newsletter or blog.
18. How we present the present-day family to the future family.
19. Hunting, fishing and vintage rods and rifles in our family history.
20. In a new country – adaptation, hardships, settler time.
21. My ancestor was a suffragette.
22. Our family and music.
23. Possible writing by the teenager of their research findings could be selected.
24. Schooling in one hundred years of family.
25. Societal changes women in the family coped with over four generations.
26. Sports in 150 years of family.
27. The story of our ancestors' kitchens.
28. The Teenage Detective: Solving Family History Puzzles.
29. Tracing family immigration – research and results.
30. Wars and our family involvement.
31. What Armistice Day means to our family.

Consider discussing your teenagers' research activities with their teachers and possible publication. A teacher or mentor may provide a note of support with the teenager's initial enquiry seeking publication.

The teenager may now be engaged in a research adventure that yields new and possibly intriguing information. They could take the lead in starting a family newsletter, noted earlier, which informs readers of family research modes and results, raises questions, seeks fellow researchers and has small-scale biographies of ancestors. The insertion of a chart and timeline is likely to foster further interest. Perhaps a cousin may assist in the development of this newsletter. It could even grow into a blog.

Teenagers Face-to-Face with History

Young family members may find themselves facing a range of moral, political, ethical, social, and historical issues in discussions with sensitive family leaders over research findings. Consider, in the following examples, parallels of the past and present which readily lead to discussions with teenagers. Human history is irrevocably linked, even integrated, with our own family's history. In that linkage, many political and ethical situations and questions arise. The family leaders could develop a selected list of these for discussions with their teenagers:

1. In England, Catholic ancestors had their religion's observance declared illegal from 1559 to 1791. How would ancestors who were 'Roman' Catholics decide whether to keep secret observances of their faith or change religions? How would this be carried out? What if they fell in love with a Protestant? Note also the Irish Penal laws of 1695 and their impact upon Catholics in Ireland, including loss of lands. Are there situations your present-day family may face, regarding restrictions on faith?

2. Gabriel Maturin was imprisoned in the Bastille for some twenty-six years (1690–1715) for not renouncing his faith. He became badly crippled in that notorious jail. The other men captured with him died or had the worst possible mental breakdowns. What could have sustained Gabriel in that time? His wife had fought for his release and, when he was freed, he reunited with his wife and family in Holland and Britain before, eventually, living in Ireland.

3. The Irish famine lasted from 1845 to 1852. Over 1 million Irish people died. Thousands emigrated to lands such as Canada, the United States, England, Australia and New Zealand. Did any of your Irish ancestral direct line, or collateral ancestors, migrate? How do your teenagers describe the self-imposed decisions and emotions of ancestors deciding on such emigration, knowing they may never see their family in their homeland again? The following family poem, held by three generations, reflects regret at the English invasion and occupation of Ireland and of the famine.

Galway 1847

From ancestral texts of descent
in heartfelt hope I need to know
my Eyre invaders
provided sustenance

to dessicated tenants who
shrivelled in the ardent embrace of
famine or joined the silent convocation
of despair – shuffling into Galway
like anchor chains
on clog clunked coffin ships.

What clues about the Irish famine can be found by youngsters in the family? Those with an inclination towards music and literature will find prose, poetry and journal accounts, folk songs and composed songs, such as *The Fields of Athenry*, which have a direct family relevance. Given one family, hard-hit by the famine, what is their view on Trevelyan, a senior English administrator in Ireland who declared, 'the judgement of God sent the calamity to teach the Irish a lesson'? Where were Irish branches of our family before, during and after the time of the famine? Which ancestors are located on passenger lists out of Ireland in the famine years? Can the teenager research a range of sources, from nineteenth-century newspapers, census returns, available online family trees and births, marriages, and deaths?

4. If they did not own their home, or the farm, women may not have qualified for the vote. Did the electoral roll always have women included? When did women get the vote? Were any of them signatories to petitions? Are there family photographs of the 'missing' female family member? Are there school records which help? Did any retain their maiden name? Do they appear in a newspaper of the time? Is there an inclusive family tree online? How can an ancestor's maiden name be located? Work back from census returns, records in particular counties, professional registers as for educators and nurses, historical newspapers, names that have been passed down, widening your use of search engines, family history magazines and books such as Emm (Pen and Sword, 2019).

5. The women in England who were over 30 years of age and had some property were allowed in 1918 to receive the vote. Ask your teenage researcher to find out if this was the same ruling for men. How would a male ancestor feel about a female ancestor's exclusion? On what basis should men and women receive the vote equally? At the 1918 voting law it meant that approximately 4 million English women were still denied the vote but no men were excluded. Had any female ancestors participated in the suffragette movement or signed petitions for women to have voting equality? Who were they and what were their backgrounds? Did any female ancestors or members of the

wider family serve in the armed services or have special work in the war effort? What is your teenager's view on these differences which were faced by direct ancestors?

6. From 1922, the majority of Irish counties became the foundation counties of the Irish Free State but six counties became Northern Ireland, within the rule of England. Many families had branches in Ulster and in Ireland. What were the possible allegiances of our ancestors in each of these domains? What were the decisions facing politicians? What do we know of these families?

7. The United Kingdom had compulsory male military service in the Second World War. How did an ancestor of that time view this? What does your teenager believe are the various considerations that such a ruling placed upon male ancestors? Were there any conscientious objectors? One Second World War relative voluntarily enlisted in the air force, fighting in the Pacific, which meant leaving his wife and 3-year-old son. What might have been his motivation? What might have been his reservations? What might have been his wife's feelings and resultant life challenges? How can you obtain his war record? Were all the family servicemen and servicewomen of age? Did any female family members serve as nurses, factory workers or flyers? What family knowledge emerges in a search for James Allison McConnell who was the captain of an air force bomber, at the age of 22 years, shot down in 1942? Have David and Lauren, in the Royal Australian Air Force, faced similar thoughts and feelings as their air force and military ancestors?

Developing a family website may well fall in the capability range of your teenager or someone in the wider family. They can find ready guidance in the knowledge of a teacher, and friends. There are free websites that provide instruction. It is recommended that your family website has your two primary surnames in its title as this means the female and male lines are noted. You should note such words as genealogy or family history in the title or in your description.

At a follow-up and more informal family research gathering, the young members and teenagers could share their research as progress reports. Parents are not in the forefront as this is the younger ones reporting to their family. Consider:

- Facts and information found in their research to date.
- Family trees to be shared, which now have additional data.
- Photographs given out to see if the subjects or locations can be identified.

- Present-day diaries, photographs, writing and art to illustrate family life today are presented.
- Presentation of oral or visual interviews with family members and friends.
- Questions for which no answer has been obtained could be given out for advice and suggestions for renewed research.
- Quizzes could be made up by the presenters to see how much of this family history is now known.
- Sharing copies of newspaper items on ancestors always draws interest.
- The two updated timelines and family trees could be given out.

The presentation of art and written works by youngsters of their present-day life, or a diary of a typical week will show 'my life today, for family members of tomorrow'. Ensure these works have information on their compilers, with names and ages. Ensure all family members are included at the starting point of your family tree.

Now is the time to discover how your teenager could help the family tree presented online:

1. Search for information about GEDCOM, a key genealogical term which has a guiding YouTube presentation.
2. Which sites will we explore for optimal family tree placement? Check on family tree software commercial aids, to present your tree and information, such as TreeView and FamilyTree Maker. MyHeritage must be checked for information and paid sites such as Ancestry.
3. Who will have access to the tree?
4. How can the tree be updated?
5. Can photographs be included?
6. Will any charges be incurred? If so, what are they?
7. Who, in our family, will be responsible for the online family tree?
8. Can copies of the tree easily be made and placed on other sites?

The presentation, and acceptance, of their research findings by young researchers is a critical consideration. Again, the parents have the quiet self-evaluation of themselves as family team leaders and their perceived realities of the venture so far:

1. Have the youngsters had the most appropriate assistance, guidance and direction?
2. Have they been assisted to best take their opportunity to present their findings?
3. How have their results been accepted?

4. How has the family history research involved each youngster, including teenagers?
5. Were they genuinely or dutifully engaged?
6. What have been the gains in the family through this?
7. What have been the gains for the individuals?
8. What would we change in our process?
9. How can the younger ones move on relatively freely from what they have done?
10. What did they find easy, difficult or boring?
11. What cooperation did you see?
12. Were siblings involved in joint research?

Teenage ventures often have underpinnings of self-education and an enhanced understanding of social history. History teachers could readily build upon this, as could virtually any elementary or high school teacher. It is to this context of self-education and formal education, with the potential for an enhanced understanding of social history, of family history and education, that the focus now turns, with avenues for home and school to draw together.

Chapter 8

HOME AND SCHOOL: FAMILY HISTORY AND FAMILY EDUCATION

The educational value of family history research has six-fold riches:

1. Self-education for the researcher learning technical skills and search methods.
2. The enhancement of various fields of knowledge and curricula.
3. The learner drawing upon wise and knowledgeable teaching, at home and at school.
4. The home-school link enhancing home-school relations.
5. The educator has varied opportunities for enhancing student learning.
6. The young researcher opens teacher awareness of education possibilities.

In school, some associations of family and history may be informal, some may arise in certain class study contexts and some will be framed in specific subject studies. Beyond history-orientated studies, creative thinking by parents and teachers could lead to student's artwork, music composition, metalwork, woodwork, handcrafts, or domestic science and cooking initiatives relating to past times.

The teacher will find online sites that provide advice for family history in the classroom and genealogy in school studies. These diverse sites range, for example, from 'Genealogy in the Classroom' (Victoria Genealogical Society in Canada) to the History in Schools site where Joe Jelen writes on students 'Discovering History Through Genealogical Research'.

Teachers and parents can note certain organisations seeking information on innovative projects. The International Bomber Command Centre in

London has been seeking information on airmen and airwomen. Here is where a knowledgeable teacher could have Gillian or Matt, Sarah-Jane or Blair engaging on family history research for an established historical organisation at **losses@internationalbcc.co.uk** to send them information on their great-grandfather's cousin, the one shot down as a 22-year-old bomber captain in the Second World War. They could send photographs taken by their grandfather and Sophia and Toby's father when they visited the war grave in Valenciennes. There is much scope for educators and families to jointly produce enriching materials for archives and specialist organisations.

The author's education career began as the sole teacher in a remote rural primary (elementary) school with all class levels. The 5-year-olds and 6-year-olds sometimes made weekly drawings and simple diaries for their grandparents, who lived elsewhere. Teaching at university level, his professorial level supervision of doctoral theses included those with strong personal and historical dimensions. At every level of lecturing, in such papers as leadership, management, school curriculum, sport history, sport and society, coaching and teaching methods there were opportunities and positive student responses in engaging with some aspect of family history. Students noted in their assessment of the lecturer that they felt more of personal link and interest in such papers because they had an unexpected but extra dimension of personal relevance. Educators at all levels could consider the following opportunities in varied subject areas at various educational levels:

1. A diary from the past, especially of a past event.
2. Agriculture and farming practice studies.
3. A timeline of history and ancestors linked with that timeline.
4. An immigration diary or journal.
5. Art opportunities.
6. Assisting children to have research projects in print or online.
7. Biology lessons linked to families' DNA.
8. Blog creation.
9. Carpentry of past generations.
10. Civic, academic, trade, governmental and royal recognition.
11. Clothing through a selected era.
12. Compiling a map of the country you live in and placing ancestors on the map.
13. Compiling a world map of family linkages.
14. Composing a piece of music from an ancestor's era; researching a musical ancestor.

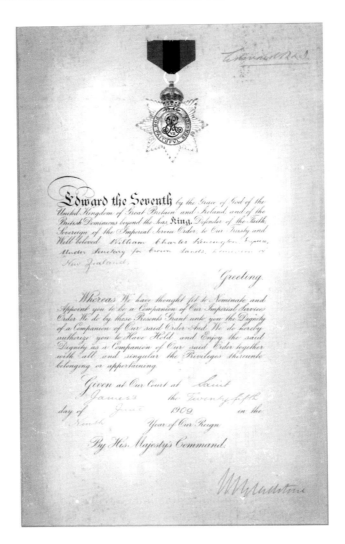

King Edward the Seventh award of the Imperial Service Order to William Charles Kensington 25 June 1909.

15. Composing music for creative presentations.
16. Constructing a family tree.
17. Cooking class with past era family recipes.
18. Creative narratives.
19. Dance creation of ancestor happenings or learning dances of yesteryear.
20. Drama creations related to past family members and past family occurrences.
21. Empire expansion studies.
22. English, or any curriculum area e.g. talks, essays, debates, creative writing.
23. Family homes through the ages.
24. Family tradition presentations.
25. Fashion boardwalk presentation of student creativity.
26. Fashion through the ages.
27. Feminine perspectives.
28. Finding an ancestor linked with the period of history being studied.
29. Finding competitions for creative writing or students' genealogical research.
30. Folklore of stories, children, songs and singing games.
31. Handcraft opportunities.
32. Handmade clothing or creative crafts of bygone days.
33. Having specialist raconteurs and engaging family historians speak to the class.
34. Historical events and historical vignettes.
35. Homeplace history.
36. Home studies, woodwork, metalwork or cooking activities in ancestors' lives.
37. Illustrating a significant episode in (family) history.
38. Interviewing.
39. Invaders and indigenous peoples.
40. Land use over time.
41. Leadership and management studies.
42. Learning a new language.
43. Learning to research and extend research skills.
44. Learning to use social media and online sources.
45. Linking with special days, e.g. VE Day, Anzac Day, Memorial Day, Mothers' Day.
46. Linking field trips with students' family history.
47. Making an ancient tool or implement by hand.
48. Making field visits, such as to a museum of local history or machinery of the past.

49. Mapping.
50. Medical beliefs and practices in past generations.
51. Music composition, song research and searches for music of ancestral days.
52. Music history, whether classical, jazz, popular or any genre.
53. Navigation through the centuries.
54. Now Here's A Great Ancestor Dude!
55. Online research by the teacher seeking home-school interactive topics and study.
56. Planning jointly with another subject or differing grade level teacher.
57. Poetry and prose: of past eras and by the present students.
58. Providing guidance for family-related historical eras and happenings.
59. Public speaking, in school and beyond, e.g. local history or genealogical group.
60. Recipe compilation.
61. Religion and the family's history, particularly in a church school subject.
62. Researching a piece of family memorabilia.
63. Researching ancestors' military encounters.
64. Research skills enhancement.
65. Scientific beliefs in the past generations.
66. Seminar or oral presentations to school, local interest groups or conferences.
67. Setting out a family tree.
68. Sociology studies at university could relate to virtually any item on this list.
69. Sport history at senior school or university level.
70. Student selected assignments such as immigration, the arts in our family, war.
71. Teachers' inter-class programme e.g. family history, 50 Years of School.
72. Teaching games and sports of past eras.
73. Team development.
74. Thesis writing upon virtually any aspect of genealogy.
75. Tourism studies.
76. Toys, games and skipping rhymes.
77. Using a university subject to link with family history perspectives.
78. Using drama.
79. Using searches of genealogical sites to develop technology research skills.
80. Woodwork or metalwork replications.
81. Writing a biography.

82. Writing for publication.
83. Writing poetry, prose, fact or fiction to bring a focus upon an ancestor.
84. Writing up interviews, field trip reports, research or special topics.

Parents can borrow school curricula and check for areas of learning which could fit with their children's research and expression. They should inform teachers of the young ones' engagement with family research and discuss possible family history research projects with teachers to see if any could fit schoolwork, skills acquisition, a class project, optional studies or curriculum areas such as English, Music, Social Studies, Sport, Homecrafts, Physical Education, Art, 'Home Science', Geography or History. Perhaps parents may email the teacher with questions they would like to discuss at the forthcoming parent-teacher meetings. Caring teachers will respond positively to hearing of greater self-confidence, research skills acquisition and new interests in their pupil.

A major bonus of locating the cemeteries in which our forebears are buried is the increase in our geographical and historical knowledge. There are wonderful results when a child, or any researcher, finds the name and place where their ancestor died, then searches online for the nearest cemeteries. Wonderful information on the family may be on the locatable tombstone on the cemetery site because some thousands of cemeteries can be accessed online. These could be located on your family-constructed maps and feature in self-chosen assignments in history, social studies or geography.

Our contemporary view of the past is shaped, to varying degrees, by our family's interpretations of the past. The possession of family diaries, letters, recognition through awards, creative memorabilia and newspaper records bring a fuller understanding of the era in which ancestors lived. A list of family history dates given to children for the months of March, April and May does not inform them on the season (which may be spring for some family forebears yet autumn or fall for others) but is made meaningful with observation, scents, weather reports, literature, diaries, chores, clothing, and family activity recorded in factual and creative works. So it is with our predecessors – moving beyond facts of dates and data to learn about them as people of an era, as people with locations, lives and roles in histories of the times and history of our family.

Ideas for essays, stories, poetry, factual writing and creative narratives arising during, or subsequent to, the family history research can be given by parents *and* teachers. The older children facing high school entry may now gain from discussions on which optional subjects they might take at high school, having developed an interest in history or geography or the study of a foreign language.

Teachers and parents wishing to learn about an example of a remarkable home-school family history initiative should check **https://www.duchas.ie/en** to read about the 1937–1939 initiative in Ireland of some 5,000 primary schools exploring traditions, games and customs of parents, grandparents and ancestors. The diverse linkages of politics, social history and geography require sensitive teaching. Consider the implications, for example, of teaching slavery or imperial expansion to a class in which students may know of their indigenous forebears, their ancestor slave owner, family in the military or the overseas settlement of ancestors.

Teachers and parents will see opportunities to help their students increase their research skills and organise and manage their research results. Deductive reasoning skills will be enhanced through carefully planned classroom activities and pupil-teacher interaction. Family history studies in any subject will, when taught by a skilled teacher, stimulate higher thinking skills. The 'difficult student' can change through being matched with a stimulating topic by an empathetic teacher.

History is, arguably, the most relevant subject for students aware of their family history. Imagine students studying a history component from the following diverse samples:

- Anzac Day in Australia and New Zealand
- Bastille
- Boxer Rebellion
- British Empire
- Brontë Sisters
- Charles Dickens
- Civil War
- Colonial periods
- Commonwealth Graves Commission
- Computer technology
- East India Company
- Elizabeth I
- English occupation of Ireland
- Fashion
- First international netball game or England-Australia cricket test
- First World War
- Florence Nightingale
- Frances Drake

- Genes and DNA
- Home life
- Huguenots
- Industrial Revolution
- Inventions and their impact
- Ireland Independence
- Irish diaspora
- Irish famine
- Lacrosse
- Major natural disasters
- *Mayflower*
- Owen Gwynedd
- Royalty
- Scotland-England political relations
- Second World War
- Shakespeare's plays
- Social history of 1960s
- Suffragettes
- Toys
- Travel and transport: Wright brothers, Earhart, bridge-building, trains, bicycles etc.
- USA Civil War
- Vietnam War
- Votes for all citizens
- War of Independence

Students could write an essay, construct a visual presentation, make a videotaped documentary or stage drama or present an insightful and creatively compiled timeline. These are brought to life by students drawing upon their heritage links to the topic. Cleo, as a young primary school pupil, completely unaware of the Anzac Poem written in her family half a century before, was awarded the top award in her school for her poem for Anzac Day, the most sacred war memories day in New Zealand. She was well aware her uncle and grandfather had visited Flanders and the First World War battlefields and that her Uncle Kit had also been to Gallipoli, where one of the family was killed. The child has the family identity in remembrance and has qualities of her direct family line; her poem follows that of her grandfather's here:

Flanders Fields
by Robin McConnell

Flanders fields enfold our loss
where Anzac youth still lie,
Flagged by poppies in the spring
beneath a northern sky,
But every April, every year,
their souls in Flanders roam
To pick those blood-red poppies
and bring those poppies home.

ANZAC Day Poppies
by Cleo Zipfel, aged 10 years.

From the rich soil
to the red petal
we will never
forget that time
when,
brown and white,
we fought,
losing the ones
we loved.

When we look back
there,
Then look around
here
the difference is huge,
So, on the twenty-fifth
The poppies again will bloom.

Our Eyre family ancestors illustrate the British occupation of Irish land. Our De la Porte, Garrigue, Plumail and Maturin ancestors bring a vivid illustration of the repression of Protestants in France and the Huguenots escaping to the British Isles.

Our family's records of their direct ancestor, Gabriel Maturin (1638–1718), being confined to a crippling twenty-six years in the Bastille, and then reuniting with his wife and family, is more gripping than any history lesson dutifully presented in an unexciting classroom. Maya talking

1724 will of Rachel Garrigue Maturin, widow of Gabriel. Rachel died 19 January 1731.

to her form, history or music class about Maturin, Swift and Handel would bring reality and genuine interest in *Messiah* at Christmas time. A sensitive teacher could have Maya write an account for a Christmas publication, linking family and history.

A range of newspaper reports, immigration records, military sources and settler arrivals illustrate the British Empire expansion and its impact upon indigenous peoples. The Kenny officers in the Seventy-third Regiment (73 Regt), East India Company military, the Fencibles in 1847 to New Zealand and the death of Richard Augustus Clay Watson (1783–1824) illustrate British efforts at expansion and, arguably, indigenous subjection.

One can readily imagine the pride voiced by one young researcher when she discovered her direct ancestor had signed a suffragette petition. What had persuaded this ancestor, in her conventional and very socially acceptable family of the time, to take this decisive public action? The search then began to learn more from any family letters that could be found, for accounts of suffragette meetings in the locality and to add to the timelines.

An oral interview with an elder in the family who fought in the Falklands brings an underpinning reality to a classroom's historical accounts. The present generation can, comparatively readily, be interviewed on their years during the period of the Vietnamese War. 'Did you and Grandad *really* protest in the street, Grandma? What happened?' Every family has someone who lived in those eras, who is a link with history lessons on the subject.

One family story from an Irish ancestor will evoke, for generations, the family's traditional account of the tragic Croke Park day in Dublin, 21 November 1920. British soldiers, in the War of Independence in Ireland, opened fire on the crowd who were watching a major Gaelic Football match at Croke Park. This heartfelt day was passed down with art, newspaper accounts, a diary and prose.

A family custom passed down a world away from Ireland explains a meal tradition which originated in their homeland's famine period. This could be illustrated by children engaged in the current family history project who have learned of the famine affecting their family and consequent emigration of family as part of the Irish diaspora. Every Sunday, in faraway Dunedin, the head of an Irish family branch kept, for decades, a family covenant by setting one spare place for a stranger who might call needing a meal; a legacy of parental practice, framed in famine, which was buried by his Antipodean family along with his Ballymoney burr. The practice has ceased. The family memory has not.

Art or music can have lasting contributions within a family. Imagine the emotions and lasting impact through family generations of certain creations that link irrevocably with family history. An example is the musical composition by Maya, as a 10-year-old harp player. She took a poem written by one of her direct ancestors for his wife, on their wedding night, and composed a touching melody that keep the words and occasion alive for her descendants. In generations to come the legacy would be noted. Who composed this? Who wrote the lyrics? Why was it written? Who put the tune to the words? What is our link with her? Can we obtain a copy of the marriage certificate? What consequent research could it lead to? Can Maya be interviewed about this and the interview passed down with the music?

Parents can raise with teachers the 'direct family line' approach with which their school children have been engaged at home. This could be done in standard 'meet the teacher' appointments, in parent-teacher interviews and in correspondence with the school. History, geography and all subject teachers can find a way to expand upon the home-school linkages by recognising appropriate subject content or assignments drawn from, and connecting with, the family history being researched by their students. It is understandable that some parents may feel they have a lack of knowledge of educational matters and may be reluctant to ask teachers about possible home-school learning linkages. However, remember that teachers respond to genuine interest in their work and appreciate recognition of their professional roles.

Every student, regardless of what their teacher thinks of their ability, could write, draw or compose an account of the time of the Covid-19 pandemic. This would draw family history and education into a personal unity of learning and family history. There is always opportunity for seizing the time, fostering valued elements of individual learning and finding flexibility in the student's selection of an assignment topic that is in accord with the teacher's curriculum overview and broader education goals. We close the classroom door now, with the teacher intriguing their students by recounting stories from their own family history.

Chapter 9

CREATIVELY RECORDING YOUR OWN FAMILY HISTORY

The recording of your family history is a marked reminder to have a very capable organisation of research and research files from the beginning of the family venture. How then, can we draw upon these for the best record, for descendants, of the results of our research and the presentation of our family today?

Writing a Family Book
A family history book for creatively recording your family's history presents its own demands. Check online as there is a massive range of helpful material for the discerning researcher! What is your family book's purpose? What is the best structure for this book? Will the book be chronological in terms of ancestors' lives? Will it focus upon family tree branches of your direct line or will it be geographically focused? What content will be valued by later generations? How is its accuracy ensured? How will the book be financed? How many copies will we do? What is the timeframe for its compilation? Can we sell copies pre-publication? Can we find technical aids and family book writing guides online? Can we really tell a story? Utilising information on aids such as Evernote can add markedly to our recorded interviews, and organisation of family history material.

What can be an enjoyable endeavour is also a challenging experience. The family history book could be the result of all the family contributing chapters, photographs, charts and creative writing. The youngest family members can contribute photographs, diaries that illustrate their typical week, results of their research, and artworks. The older ones can provide family trees, succinct ancestor biographies and recorded interviews. Perhaps you have a section for each person in the family to write about themselves, their research and its results and anything about family history they wish to send on.

Gather the evidence for a book or online presentation that can readily be shared with all the families who share research with you. Books are wonderful sources of information – and pleasure – at family reunions. The family history book will probably have pictorial, visual and print records that add to the narrative depth of your family's history. The power of past generation diaries, scrapbook excerpts, letters, inscriptions, newspaper entries, certificates or transcripts of interviews add reality to our expressed knowledge of ancestors as people. Double-check the content, dates and statements of 'fact'. It is rare to find a family history that is completely free of error or inconsistency. Some resources could be edited and distributed to family members, with the book, as ancillary items.

Whether you make a book, detailed family trees or biographies, consider putting an ancestor's family tree chart number with their name in the print material or in the index which has individuals' full names. Perhaps the trees are foldouts or in an accompanying folder.

Printing the Family History Book

How will your family plan for the book's printing and distribution? Check sources such as MyCanvas and Blurb to find ideas for the presentation of your book. Self-publishing is a widespread activity so check sites and costs. Your town will be a good place to start, but search online for possible publishers or printers as well. Read reviews and evaluations from genuine users. Use search engines to see examples of books. Ask at your library, local newspaper and local genealogical group.

In these days of photobooks and phone use of photography we find opportunities for the formation of handmade books and home-made publications produced for future generations. Photobooks can be compiled. Some families do this annually and others do this to mark a special occasion. Scanning photographs can be learned by youngsters and they can assemble the photographs in a draft book. They will learn about photo resolution and enlarging photographs, for which they can find free guidance online. Technological advances are continually evolving. This underscores the critical use of search engines in locating up-to-date information.

Photographs offer more than a simple record of past and present family members. In a family history book, a skilful arrangement of photographs can become the heartbeat of the body of information. The enhancement of photographs brings a greater understanding of the era. Tag your photographs with the full names of persons, the date or approximate well-reasoned date and other relevant information such as the setting. Check out free sources for clarifying murky photographs and for colouring photographs that enhance their presentation and appeal. Look at MyHeritage Photo Enhancer as an example. You can save your photographs at FamilySearch. Lodge a copy of the family book with the local archive.

Cleo, at 10 years of age, is an excellent cook. She has learned recipes from her German father and grandparents. She could assemble a family history recipe book that has cross-generational recipes. This could contain traditional recipes from her other grandparents and some that she has found in outdated recipe books. Are there recipes or cooking hints that were passed down to her grandparents that could be included? Does the local charity shop have cookbooks of her grandparents' generation?

Creative and Factual Writing

If a family member has a strong interest in writing they could collect – and write – factual accounts, diaries, essays or poems related to the family (relatives, locale, lives, historical incidents). Preferably the writers could be identified and linked to a historical timeline that fits with the narrative in a family history. Maya and Sophia could assemble their creative and factual writing for an informative week depicting their lives. Some poems from an older generation would lead to questions of meaning and relevance that help youngsters of the present understand more of ancestral times, places and circumstances.

The Louth poem in the Coleman family can lead young researchers to establish the identity and lifeline of the known teacher-poet, Peadar Ó Doirnín, who connected with their Coleman forebears. The poem stimulates speculation that is converted into research questions. Who may have written it? In what era was the poem written? Who was Ó Doirnín, for whom the love of a Coleman ancestor's sister 'ambushed reason and held it hostage in his poet heart'? Young researchers learn of him teaching in a County Louth hedge school and of Protestant-Catholic divides that may not be as readily apparent in their lives today.

A family history book could be compiled of creative written and visual arts. It could include photographs of handmade crafts, garden ornaments, model wooden planes, handmade horseshoes, machines of a century ago, carvings and great-grandparents' seemingly crude dairy herd milking machines. Some present-day family members have not seen a scarecrow! Do youngsters know of a washboard, outdoor lavatory, typewriter, bicycle without gears, pens and ink, bloomers or Roman sandals, push lawnmowers, cassette recorders, garden and carpentry tools without engines, 'getting the cane' or having a record player?

The author's family, close and distant, has a tendency to leave and receive messages for others in the family. In the poem, almost indistinguishable with aged discoloration, left on the tombstone of Samuel and Margaret Coates in Kirkby Ravensworth, North Yorkshire, were unusual words: *manuhiri* and *moko*. Googled, we find they are Māori words from New Zealand meaning a visitor and a tattoo which indicates family linkage.

Kirkby Hill Church, North Yorkshire

The world turns on itself and here
i am with my great-grandfather
as manuhiri and moko
standing in the eleventh century
st peter and st felix where misty words
breathe morning service over stone
texting of samuel and margaret coates
my progeny root of ramified bones
set in english soil, yoked to yorkshire
kin in kirkby ravensworth.

Beneath the air bridge of retinue oaks
the Latin school of john dakyn
is moored at the fence where lank
grass grapples expatriate ankles
but inside church walls i inherit
curate lake coates 1665 and church
warden coates 1773 whose spirits roam
the limestone escarpment with north
riding reticence undimmed in their
restrained felicity for returning kin.

Was it a New Zealand relative who wrote this? Can we assume that one of the Coates extended family, whose ancestral roots are here in Yorkshire, was visiting from a distant home? Can a knowledgeable youngster link them with Samuel and Margaret Coates, who are their direct ancestors? Could relatives, in North Yorkshire, solve these questions? Did the church have a visitors' book that could yield a family name of the visitor? These were researched by a young family researcher who eventually solved time, place and person questions.

The author's recently discovered Story ancestry, through his biological grandfather, Bernard Samuel Story (1872–1937), led to ancestors who wrote poetry and engaged in other expressive arts. The discovery of *Carmina Silvulae pomes,* written in 1890 by Bernard's father, James Ambrose Story (1845–1910), is a collection of his written and translated poetry published in 1890. His poems had a dedication to his mother, a poem to his sister on her ninth birthday and a poem to his child born in 1869. Discovering facts about these members of an ancestor's immediate family gains meaning when the personal descriptions in writing underscore those facts.

Children readily experiment with italic and script-writing inks and pens. They soon appreciate the challenges of handwriting experienced by their grandparents using nib pens and inks for cursive handwriting. Some of the family history book could be written in such handwriting. KidZonews will show young researchers some cursive writing ideas and tracing. Some families may even have copybooks passed down from their forebears.

A book could have contributions from different branches of the family line. This could have a common first section, with ancestors listed who are directly linked to each of the family trees that are subsequently described. Search again for self-publishing possibilities. Explore sites such as Blurb and Bookemon. One researcher relation suggested checking MyCanvas. Do not rush your decision on the book.

Compiling Ancestor Biographies

A set of present or past family members' biographies can be compiled by family members. Draw upon family discoveries from sources such as census, electoral rolls, newspaper archives, the major genealogical sites noted in this book and online family trees. The historical setting for each biography adds to understandings of them. Perhaps there are land records and local histories that deepen the portrayal. Can you create informative maps showing ancestral movement and places of living? Set the subject person in a visual family tree at the start of your biography. What photographs, letters, artworks or memorabilia add to this? Is there, by any chance, an oral record of this person anywhere? If you are planning a reunion, as outlined in Chapter 10, then hold off decisions until then and have informed discussions on what book or family memory creation is preferred.

National archives, a national library, media archives, county or state or province archives may have biographies, photographs or interviews of an ancestor. Locate these and acknowledge their holder. Present-day members of the family could be interviewed, Skype or Facetime, face-to-face. These interviews become part of the family's oral history and should have transcriptions. Lodge copies of your key material with the local archives.

Grandparent Legacies

Treat grandparents to the evolving findings of your family research. Perhaps you stage an exhibition for grandparents and the older generations to show the progress and achievements of the present/recent family research adventure. This will give recognition to the findings and creations of various family members. Posters could be made of photographs, art, written pieces, family trees and memorabilia.

The elderly are especially appreciated on their family history voyage. It is hoped they will be assisted to set out their family knowledge and memories in their own quiet reflection. The value of their carefully compiling their legacy of information, often not known hitherto, lies in more than the record that will be passed to descendants. Time is, arguably, shortening its landscape for their future. The legacy that can be contributed by them to the present and the future is tangible and intangible. The care and compassion we have for our grandparents and elderly family members is enhanced with the legacy of memories they are passing on. It is important that, just as the youngest gain from compiling insights of their family today, the elderly gain in mental stimulation, feelings of self-worth and the regard of family members as they quietly compile their memories and knowledge of family history. Consider the intrinsic value in which the following apply to our grandparents' contemplative and creative legacies:

- Creating for 'our selves' is creating for 'other selves'.
- Creating for 'other selves' is creating for 'our selves'.
- It opens the knowledge base of those living now.
- It underscores to family that they are living now and in the future.
- It reinforces and uplifts our regard for them and their experiences.
- It improves the quality of life for elderly *and* younger selves.
- It reduces depression and stress.
- It is mentally stimulating and mentally healthy.
- It can help fight dementia.
- It can enhance family relationships and interpersonal bonds.
- It enhances self-esteem as a family member.
- It is a pleasurable pursuit.

For our grandparents, writing their personal life history is a recognition of the past, a boon to their present and their gift to the future. Do not place pressure upon them but support their unique efforts of their legacy.

Objects and Subjects

In creatively recording one's family history the ideas come from diverse stimuli. One family branch enjoys going to charity shops, antique shops, second-hand and gift shops. They do this, in part, to find materials that link to earlier years and lifestyles of parents, grandparents and earlier family members. They get ideas for making lasting gifts and innovative family history materials, which they enjoy in the present and pass on to the future. Their finds have included:

- Cameras, daguerreotypes, dioramas and projectors
- Childhood comics and books
- Christmas materials
- Clean and trendy used clothes that can have printed messages, ancestor names or a branch of the family tree put on them
- Clothing of past eras
- Cooking equipment
- Fountain pens and cursive writing sets
- Games
- Magnets with photographs on them
- Model cars from an earlier family era
- Olde Worlde notebooks and diaries
- Picture and photo frames that can rehouse an image of an ancestor
- Postcards of places linked with the family
- Recipe books from past decades
- School books, pupils' workbooks and prescribed texts from past times
- Song and music collections of past days
- Sports equipment
- Time pieces
- Tools
- Toys
- Vintage equipment, ranging from typewriters to hand planes to handbells
- Washboards

Some of the finds were bought for present-day pleasure, but some were treated as special because they illustrated past lifetimes and have been retained for that reason. The pleasurable browsing led to children using old tools, writing diary entries about the discovery, making posters of ancestors with a purchased object of the time, replicating vintage-type photographs, cursively writing accounts of daily life, wearing dated clothing, making collections of *Classics Illustrated* comics, learning to use an abacus and playing backyard sport with dated and often awkward gear.

There are stimulating activities that illustrate adventurous dimensions of the research. Consider how the research findings obtained by family members of all ages add to their sense of enjoyment when they creatively engage in having key facts, ancestors, family history dates, photographs or family tree extracts placed on coffee mugs, stationery, caps, pictures on magnets, placemats or coasters, T-shirts, paperweights, tea towels or wall hangings. Check out local souvenir shops for ideas. Consider one of these created with the image of a known direct ancestors.

Father and son are rare photos.

Imagine the impact of having youngsters' creative expressions of their genealogy and findings made into gift posters. The creative perspectives of family history fit with the realities of research findings, whether kept as book online storage, preserved files, packaged records or any other form of recording for future generations.

Chapter 10

MOVING FORWARD WITH YOUR OWN FAMILY HISTORY

The preceding chapter introduced a range of creative actions that we now take into the family's future. Concomitant with the definition that underpins this book, that *family history is a history of the direct family in the past and in the present – recorded for the future,* is the present family's research goal of assembling today's material for tomorrow's generations. It is timely now to consider how the family's assembled records, knowledge and activities results will best be handed on to our descendants.

Moving forward with your own family history is a challenge *and* an immensely rewarding process for the family. Today's children will be tomorrow's adult bearers of family knowledge and then their dependants and descendants will add further knowledge and records as they, in turn, take your family history further into the future. Your youngsters and your parents have participated in this family history adventure with you. What do they want to take forward? How do they want to take it forward?

Families enjoy the challenge of constructing and storing information in a time capsule. This capsule may have multiple copies, perhaps one for each current family member. It might be assembled and stored online, distributed on social media to family or placed on DVDs or USB sticks or in other computer modes of storage. It could include a book that recounts the research adventure, the participants and the attractive presentation of research results. Some time capsules get opened a decade later or even annually. The time capsule discussed here is one that goes to the next generation.

A physical time capsule appeals to young family members. Use search engines to locate online recommendations for the best container, how to avoid records and photographs becoming discoloured and the special paper to use. Take time to locate the best box or waterproof container. Search for guidance on protecting photographs, paper and objects. Consider making copies on quality acid-free paper and the lasting ways to copy or photograph newspaper clippings. It is advisable not to use aids such as paper clips, rubber bands or sticky tape as they deteriorate over time. Ask at your library, museum, archives or family history centre for their recommendations. One family has wide pieces of sealed piping for their capsule, but a plastic box is popular.

The capsules could be illustrated on the outside by young family members. Each of the author's grandchildren has a named special box progressively containing material, which they will receive in their teens. The sides of such boxes will be illustrated. The time capsule contents could include some of the following keepsakes.

- Accounts of family history research undertaken and its results
- Appropriate mementos
- Autograph books
- Cemetery locations and photographs
- Charts of family trees
- Children's artwork
- Coats of Arms and pedigrees

A very early art work by Toby, kept in his time capsule box.

- Copies of certificates and awards
- Copies of official records such as birth, marriage and death certificates; census returns; tax returns; home purchase statements; and rates accounts
- Details of the current family
- Diaries of a week
- DNA results
- Family timelines
- Grandparents' records, memories and memorabilia
- Historical timelines
- Home address and photographs
- Insurance records
- Interviews with family members about their current lives
- Letters from the past and present and letters to future descendants
- Licences: driving and special work
- Maps showing family locations nationally and worldwide
- Meet our Family
- Military records
- Newspaper articles
- Original writing, dance and art
- Pictures of the week's activities
- Questionnaires completed by each of the family
- Photographs, carefully identified to establish identity and places
- Printouts from historical newspapers

A very early artwork by Cleo, kept in her time capsule box.

- School records
- Taxation returns
- Tickets to favourite events
- Unsolved family mysteries as challenges for the next generation to solve
- Visitor Books
- Wedding invitations, programmes, guest lists and photographs
- Wills

One young family team member wrote a letter to an ancestor telling of life in the present and how they enjoyed researching that direct line person.

An action that can appeal to many youngsters is writing a letter to their future selves. This could have a week's diary attached, art, illustrations and mention of friends and family. They could also record school life, weekly life, sport, music, church, dancing, cultural commitments and life at home. Photographs can be included. Imagine children writing about their own lives, sealing and futureproofing these and placing them in their own time capsule. Their letters could explain the research that the youngsters had undertaken and writing of their dreams for their future selves. These could be put in some special place to be opened, say, in ten or twenty years.

Norman Charles Kensington (1878– 1957) who, despite formal attire, may be singing 'Sitting in the Kennel with the Bulldog Pup'.

The decision on who shall receive a time capsule will be based upon close relationships. Each of the children in the present family would have a time capsule.

Understandably, there is always consideration on whether the capsule will be an appropriate gift for wider family members. Can it be added to in subsequent years? It is re-emphasised it is vital to check the sites that offer guidance on preserving family archival material. *Family Tree Magazine* should be checked.

Leaving letters around the world for descendants has always been a family interest of ours. Travelling in Great Britain and internationally,

A very early artwork, at 5 years old by Maya, kept in her time capsule box.

notes have been left for descendants in a range of locations that have strong family connections. Each has been placed in a secure private niche or location where it might be found by a descendant. The letters contained information about the location, its relevance to our family's history and sometimes a map or notes on ancestors from that place. Each letter has been written to a descendant and lists have been kept of these overseas left letter locations. One example is a letter hidden in the abandoned cowshed of a New Zealand farm. Another was left in a school in Canberra, and one at Worton, Wiltshire, where Charles Snell Kensington had given land and money for the church. Coates, in Gayles, Yorkshire, Watson in Southwell, Jones in Llanystumdwy and Maturin in Dublin generated concealed messages also.

Perhaps the family moves forward with its family history by planning a special countrywide holiday that encompasses key family locations but has adventure overtones with young ones' interests in mind. The idea of an over-planned or repetitive series of days on holiday will surely turn boys and girls off the interest that family research can have. A stimulation to family research comes with well-planned holidays or adventure trails that have a focus upon parents' earlier lives, grandparents' lives, interesting ancestors and puzzles and games. Consider having your older children, possibly in conjunction with grandparents, plan such a trip. The holiday could include key family places, museums or participatory historical sites and have a brief relevant presentation by one family member at each place. Do have a balance in this expedition!

With each of the family having a copy of the family map, track out a sequence of places to visit and prepare brief facts for each place. You may compile a range of maps. These could show where the family lived, and the schools attended. Perhaps future generations will add data to these maps. A basic records assemblage of ancestors' births, marriages and deaths has long been done and these now bear tangible fruit. Searches of newspapers archives may have yielded names and places. Local news items may have been found that have mentioned the family, schools attended, achievements, family events that occurred and certain family notices. Children enjoy standing where their parents and/or grandparents grew up. The author's children delighted in being at the now overgrown farm where their father, their aunt and their uncles had been children.

One of the family researchers will have written to schools, weeks prior to the family's voyage of exploration, to seek confirmation or otherwise on family members having been pupils and to obtain a copy of their

What was the location and address of this family home in 1953?

enrolment details. These often give the student's residential address, dates of enrolment and departure from the school and may indicate where the student was going after the school years finished. Your family now has assembled maps and timelines and data. After this 'once in a lifetime' family exploration, who will update these, add to them and distribute them to family members? Some special copies could be made for grandparents and significant other family members. Take a brief biography of each ancestor to the place associated with them.

The material collected in the family history researching will markedly assist specific considerations of where to go on the family history 'detective journey' or holiday. Specific examples of places to visit on a family expedition are wide-ranging.

- Buildings associated with family activity, e.g. dancehall, sport ground, Masons, clubs
- Cemeteries with family members buried there
- Churches attended
- Grandparent towns and occupation sites
- Historical and heritage sites, some of which run holiday and education programmes
- Homes lived in
- Locations of friends from earlier days and letters from them
- Museums with relevant displays, e.g. 'This is the same car as Grandpa had.'
- Places associated with a specific aspect of family life
- Relatives to be visited
- School(s) to be seen
- Significant social or recreational areas
- Streets, parks or town places named after an ancestor
- The family farm, workplace or past business
- Towns where a parent or ancestor was born, married or died
- Where special family happenings occurred
- Where parents first lived
- Work and employment sites

If the family has a strong cultural or ethnic heritage then youngsters should be taught the protocol for visiting relatives or attending a cultural centre with which their family has allegiance. Each stop on your voyage of discovery could have a presentation by a family member who has researched a particular aspect of that stopping place. The able young researcher can prepare for their stop by having information, quizzes and discussions the night before, succinct biographies, the visible family tree and games with family members featured, etc. Envisage an imaginative board game with family ancestors and family history facts; a family timeline to sort out; a map or timeline with names to be entered and, perhaps, a game such as 'True or False'. Photographs of the family member(s) to be featured the next day or who were featured today can be shared.

The author's visit to his Welsh family locales was especially moving. Criccieth and Holyhead then led to Llanystumdwy, each with special associations with forebears. Llanystumdwy was illustrative of the points above as it brought strong links through many past family markers. The graves of Anwyl and Jones ancestors were chronicled in a rare book discovered in a local second-hand bookshop, *Gleanings from God's Acre* by J. Jones (1903, Richard Jones), which resonates with emotion and factual information. Such is what may happen on your well-prepared family tour that evokes special meaning and lasting memories.

Parents and grandparents often keep early paintings and craftworks created by their younger family members. These have a sentimental value of course but also bring perspectives on their life lived and the impact of people and surroundings upon them. Ancestors may be found whose handmade artefacts or gifted creations have been handed down with their transferred touch of generations. Looking at family memorabilia should ensure the history of their family importance and knowledge of the creator are recorded.

The heirlooms and memorabilia not given to living family members should be carefully kept, decisions made on who will receive them, pricing done for possible insurance, and storage decisions made. A short history of the heirloom's importance in the family and its particular link to an ancestor must be recorded with the heirloom.

The author has a nephew serving in the air force. His cousins decided that he should receive the nineteenth-century military medal awarded to their great-great-great-great-grandfather. An academic gown from one older family member has become a goal to wear for at least one young family member when she graduates. A family member, with terminal illness, wrote letters to be given to her daughters when they graduated.

Compile a history of the family's engagement in a particular sphere of life in which they were engaged for, say, at least three generations, e.g. shopkeeping, farming, industry, military services, public service, nursing, education, church, schools, occupations, creativity, business ownership and family ventures.

Over the years, photographic books of the year, as undertaken by the author's daughter and daughter-in-law, have provided the family with enjoyable visual records of their year's events. The books are printed in full colour, sometimes with soft covers and sometimes with hardcovers. With an eye on the future from the present, variations of such books can provide an update of particularly relevant interesting family history each year, along with a section on the year just completed. See, again, Chapter 8, where your family's more substantial family history book is considered.

Newspaper archives add to our family knowledge. English newspapers in the early nineteenth century noted the ancestor who inherited a Tobago estate with slaves upon it. This still causes enervating discussions of legal, ethical and civic considerations in his present-day descendants.

The pleasure the youngest of the family can have in their knowledge of their ancestry is reflected in a 1984 diary in which five fourth cousins featured:

> The five children, all under 15 years of age, came running out of an antique shop declaring with glee that they had found the riding boots of their great-great-great-great-grandfather, John Larkin Kensington! They were gleeful, as the boots they found had the initials JLK in them. They knew the boots were not his but loved the humour with which they were engulfed – humour and sharing that would not have been possible if they did not know their family history, for JLK had died in Tobago in 1837.

A family blog should be considered. This is relatively straightforward and the family member responsible for it could readily Google advisory sources and learn from other's blogs. Try **www.blogger.com** or other sites found with key words.

Coats of Arms

Were there coats of arms in your family? Some families develop a strong interest in the family's real or alleged right to a coat of arms. This may be a costly formal journey. Research the rights to bear arms and information required for submission to the College of Arms, for example. In USA there is the American College of Heraldry.

Is there a family motto? An enjoyable and informative creative effort is that of the children constructing their own version of a family coat of arms. To do this, with maximum impact, they need to understand the basic purpose of a coat of arms and how family interests, achievements and recognition of certain ancestors and their deeds or 'social class' led to the granting of arms. Capable children could search the list of their ancestral family's surnames to see if any name has an associated coat of arms. There is often a fascination with learning the meaning of arms' symbols, which are explained online, and constructing your own family coat of arms.

The family needs to understand that some persons, families and commercial enterprises have constructed their own 'coats of arms' without the approval of the Herald or official bodies so beware of paying commercial groups who simply provide a coat of arms for your name – at your expense and not validated for you by, say, the College of Arms. The informative article by Sharon Combs Bennett (January–February 2018) is worthy of attention. The author's family has hand-painted 'coats of arms' of Kensington and De la Porte that are yet to be verified. The author's son or daughter or a nephew or niece could follow up on the direct lineage rights to the Maturin coat of arms.

Coat of Arms in Kensington family memorabilia. To be pursued!

Organising storage of the family history material prompts a check of family history software sites. Range over Backupmytree.com, Evernote (organising and retaining your files, retaining audio-visual material), Dropbox and WordPress (develop your own family history website). Check for free software. See Paton (2021) for ideas on sharing and preserving stories.

Family Reunion

Results of the family history research adventure lead readily to a family get-together or reunion. Discuss this with members of the wider family. Look ahead to any previously unnoticed anniversary that is forthcoming or a date upon which a significant family event occurred – the family research adventure could have that commemorative date as a target for a family reunion or get-together. The family newsletter could suggest a choice of dates. The special day could be one related to birth or marriage, graduation, an award received, arrival in a new country, a military engagement, an important career appointment or a significant social occasion. How will this be marked? Who will attend? Check reunion messages online and in newspapers. Locate the *Reunions Magazine* to see ideas and actions to consider. Discuss costs and how these will be handled. How will the elderly family members be part of this?

The reunion could mark the successful conclusion of Phase One of your family's research adventure. You have traced your direct family history with your whole family. A Phase Two could come from individuals who will continue to research, some who move to sporadic research and some who shift their emphases to present-day material for the time capsule. Some may not wish to sustain their family history research. There will still be a sharing of information within the family. The reunion becomes the culmination, in many ways, of that Phase One 'all-in' family research. It has the stimulation of sharing, meeting relatives and reinforcing the concept of 'whole-family'. Consider an aid such as Periscope, **www. periscope.tv**, to make the reunion real for the absentees.

Who will organise the day? Can it be held at a location that has a strong family connection? All ages could engage in the consideration of organisational possibilities. This day could then be drafted by teenagers who consider the planning checklist for full family participation, noting family members who will be associated with a particular task or responsibility. The list indicates considerations in the planning:

1. Search online for articles and guidance on holding a family reunion.
2. Double-check this list with other family members.
3. What is the purpose of the reunion?
4. Decide mutually on a location and date well ahead, such as in six months or a year.
5. What family history link is there with the date(s) proposed?
6. How will the day be recorded?
7. Ensure full compliance with local, regional or governmental health requirements.
8. Send out a communication of initial information and suggestions. Seek support from family members who would accept responsibility for some significant aspect of the reunion.
9. Gauge the support level for the proposed reunion.
10. Who will be invited?
11. What is the cut-off date for a decision on whether there are enough numbers coming to justify having the reunion?
12. What would be the decisive factors leading to considerations of cancellation or postponement of the reunion?
13. If the reunion is considered for cancellation, could it be replaced with a virtual reunion?
14. Obtain the contact details of all who could be involved and attend. A teenager could collect and collate the contact information on relatives, such as names, place in the family, addresses, emails, social media contacts and telephone numbers. Circulate these.
15. Ensure that contact details are obtained for family overseas and non-attending family members who will receive reunion information

and may be able to provide research findings and family history information for the reunion.

16. What facilities are required?
17. How many people are estimated to attend?
18. What accommodation might be needed? Organise lists and discount prices of commercial accommodation.
19. Will a genealogy publisher, local bookshop, local history or national genealogical group, library or archive wish to have a stand to show their family history material?
20. What equipment and aids will be required?
21. Are there any aural or visual interviews of an ancestor that could be a feature?
22. What provisions, leisure tables and chairs are needed?
23. Who will compile a map and provide this?
24. What family history could different branches of the family bring?
25. Is the planned date a special date in any family member's personal life?
26. What is the budget and how will this be paid for?
27. Will any family members, particularly the elderly or those with severely restricted movement, require transport or special care?
28. Will there be clean and functional lavatory and handwashing facilities?
29. Will there be ache relievers, sanitary provisions, towels, first-aid materials, rest area, a defibrillator, etc.?
30. Possible requirements for health considerations, special needs and special diets are considered.
31. Ascertain which family attendees have medical skills, qualifications or occupations.
32. Ensure one person has full information on the nearest doctor, medical centre, hospital and ambulance service. Make this person known to attendees.
33. Ensure one person has local contacts for police and emergency services such as a fire brigade. Make this person known to attendees.
34. Advise attendees of any family history compilation for sale and, preferably, have this pre-paid if they wish to receive one at the reunion.
35. Are there any local body regulations that need to be complied with?
36. Check on local requirements for fires, barbecues and rubbish/waste disposal. Will people take their rubbish home or have containers provided? Who will empty these?
37. Ensure that the invitations give an informative outline of the reunion, indicate special contributions that can be made, practical assistance

that can be given and ensure attendees bring their full family history information.

38. Give a broad account of the family's research to date. Explain that findings will be presented at the reunion.

39. Who will obtain provisions? How will this be done and paid for?

40. Practicalities of inclement weather should be double-checked. An alternative location, such as a school, church or community hall should be considered, in reserve, in case of inclement weather.

41. Give appropriate organisational responsibilities, with guidelines, to family members.

42. Carefully arrange for meals, with different branches of the family having responsibilities for meals.

43. Consider making a 'family olden days' recipe booklet available. Sell copies before or at the reunion.

44. Who will handle social media such as Facebook?

45. Arrange for identified photographs to be displayed – or have an 'identification quiz'. Have enough copies for the attendees to take home.

46. Compile a large family tree chart showing all of those attending and their forebears. Ensure that each person's name has a clear number.

47. Consider handouts on research methods, online sites to be searched and key abbreviated biographies of ancestors.

48. Have blank research forms and family tree charts freely available.

49. Will local media be informed of the reunion and invited to attend?

50. Will an attendee write an article or report for the newspaper?

51. What displays will be set up by attendees?

52. Display a large historical timeline with historical events on one line and names of ancestors on a lower line, placed appropriately. It may be easier, as one reunion found, to have the large historical timeline, with its dates and major events, and to simply place ancestors' numbers (with which they are identified on the family trees) on their relevant time of the historical timeline.

53. Games from past eras can be taught and played, such as marbles or tops.

54. Simple colouring books of ancestors and family settings could be made for children.

55. Have a large national map displayed with individual ancestor numbers. Attendees put a numbered pin on their home location and enter the number on the attached sheet of paper with their name(s) and addresses and contact details.

56. Have a session for young family members taken by older youngsters.

57. Have displays or accounts of past family members and their happenings presented for questions and answers on specific ancestors, ancestral settings, lifetime dates etc.

58. Family members present papers on one selected ancestor or family member.

59. Ensure family representatives of the wider family work on the reunion.

60. Prepare for light moments: photograph identification competitions; True or False quizzes presented by younger family members; Family History Trivia; old-time family facts to be matched with a given list of ancestors and other fun activity that someone has offered. Quiz presenters will be confirmed prior to the day.

61. Consider special breaks for family music, dancing or activity such as skipping.

62. Have name tags, numbered and colour coded, so the particular family or family line can be readily established. Ensure these are known by participants before they attend.

63. T-shirts or polo shirts could be prepared with ancestry wording. Pre-ordering and accurate sizes are critical.

64. Have attendees prepare specific accounts of a genealogy research process and results.

65. How will the organisation of the day(s) be done?

66. Introduce each person or, at least, the heads of the family branches. Consider pairing relatives, who have not previously met, who will introduce each other.

67. Locate any nearby museum to visit or which could receive local family histories.

68. One of the family could explain methods of making books, tapestry or posters of their family branch.

69. Dated home movies could be digitised and sold at the reunion.

70. One reunion asked for attendees to dress in the mode of their ancestors for the dinner.

71. Perhaps there are creative family members who would put on a dramatic or humorous sketch of some incident or person(s) from the family's past or a mock re-enactment of two family members trying to get an answer to a research question.

72. Prepare charts or posters with questions seeking information and the contact details of enquirer.

73. Display the project to create your own coat of arms.

74. Take photographs of all attending, listing names, contact details and family links.

75. Ensure a full record of the reunion is sent to those who attended and to other relevant persons, particularly any hospitalised or elderly family members who missed attending. Consider overseas family members – what they will be informed of and what they will receive.
76. How will new family information, presented at the reunion, be disseminated?
77. Will there be opportunity for attendees to provide an evaluation of the reunion?
78. Will a family branch offer to organise the next reunion?
79. Letters of thanks and appreciation will be sent promptly.

Inevitably, the family reunion is going to leave a legacy for those involved. New relationships, further research, recorded memories and shared knowledge are major steps in the whole family's journey. Time for informal socialising may prove to have been the most significant aspect of the reunion, especially as it allows for informal updates on cousins and geographically distant family.

Your return home will foster a critical focus on time capsule plans. Ensure that space is left in your family time capsule for later additions and that the next generation can add to the capsule (in whatever form it takes) or create additional time capsules to pass on. The criteria for the family should be made clear: will this capsule take past and present family history to the next generation and will the capsule provide descendants with a full set of information to stimulate their research on the family? You and your present family, especially your grandparents, are leaving a family legacy for future generations.

A warm family reunion with family coming from three countries.

The research adventure reunion draws a close to the organised first phase of your immediate family's journey. Have a special time with your family team when you celebrate and evaluate the journey and what has been achieved. Ensure records are kept and each family member receives a copy of what has been discovered. The completed time capsules are set aside but may be added to by those who engage in further research. Encourage any family member who wishes to continue with their searching.

This book began with a definition of family history centred upon the direct family line to guide the research focus. The family research had a focus upon direct ancestors but will have increasingly recognised that their family is more expansive than their direct line, that *family history is a history of the family in the past and in the present – recorded for the future.* It leaves us with every family's heartfelt echo of the challenging words that underpin the real depth of family history: *Honour the past, value the present and safeguard the future.*

Appendix I

SOURCES FOR TRACING YOUR FAMILY ANCESTRY

This appendix has a range of sites to assist family history, usually additional to those in the text. The listings in 1–4 are basic aids to any genealogical researcher and relisted here for emphasis. The appendix is a guiding sampler, as genealogical resources frequently change and search engine research is the best means of keeping up to date. The first set of highly rated international sites, noted here for in-depth genealogical searching, is generally agreed upon. Browsing the sources below will lead you to other sites and further relevant fields. It is strongly recommended that bookshops and libraries are checked for family history magazines. Online searches for family history, genealogy and history magazines bring pleasure and knowledge, often more up to date than books.

1a. Primary Family History Research Sites
- Ancestry: **www.ancestry.co.uk**
- FamilySearch: **www.familysearch.org**
- Findmypast: **www.findmypast.co.uk**
- MyHeritage: **www.myheritage.com**
- TheGenealogist: **www.thegenealogist.co.uk**

1b. Primary Family History Research Sites
- Cyndi's List: **www.cyndislist.com**
- GenealogyBank: **www.genealogybank.com**
- Genes Reunited: **www.genesreunited.co.uk**
- Geni.com: **www.geni.com**
- IGI: *See FamilySearch*
- Newspapers.com: *See Ancestry*
- RootsWeb: *See Ancestry*.

2. Free Sites

There are many free sites. Check your search engine answers to 'What is the best free genealogy site?' Some primary sites above offer free access periods. The best of free sites is FamilySearch. Try the following sampling. Check further sites in the recommended books in Chapter 2.

- Ancestry free Census Finder
- Cindi's List
- Dusty Docs
- Europeana
- Facebook
- FamilySearch
- *Family Tree Magazine*
- Findmypast
- Flickr and Flickr Commons
- Foundation for Online Genealogy
- Free UK Genealogy
- GenCircles
- General Register Office for Northern Ireland (GRONI)
- Genguide
- Genuki
- Heritage quest
- Internet Archive
- Irish Genealogy
- MooseRoots
- MyHeritage
- National Archives
- Olive Tree Genealogy
- Pinterest
- RootsChat
- RootsFinder
- RootsWeb
- Treelines
- UKBMD
- US GenWeb
- WeRelate
- Wikipedia List of Genealogical Databases
- WikiTree
- World Connect (FamilySearch)
- WorldGenWeb

3. Children and Family History

Sites, arguably, are not as plentiful as one would hope. Locate RootsWeb. Check the Cyndi's List topics at **www.cyndislist.com/kids/general/children**'s section. Use your search engine seeking 'Children and Family History' to enjoy articles, suggestions and information, and check **www.thefhguide.com/act-children.html**. See the following examples, and books by Beller, Frazel, Frisch, Greene, Niggemeyer and Resler, noted in the bibliography:

- COKidGenWeb Project
- Family Tree for Kids at **www.thefhguide.com/act-children.html**
- Family Tree Kids! Making History Fun
- Junior Genealogists
- Pinterest, from Ancestry, has Genealogy for Kids
- RootsWeb has SaskGenWeb and USGenWebKidz
- WGW for Kids at **http://www.worldgenweb.org/~wgw4kids/**
- **www.familytreemagazine.com/kids/welcome.asp**
- **www.genealogyspot.com/features/kids.htm**
- **www.genealogyspot.com/resources/kids.htm**
- **www.rootsweb.ancestry.com/~cokids**
- **www.rootsweb.ancestry.com/~usgwkidz**

4. Social Media

Do not neglect the social media sites with which you may already be familiar: Amazon; Facebook; Facetime; Pinterest; Skype; WeRelate; Twitter; WikiTree and YouTube. See **https://cyndislist.com/facebook**. Pinterest, for example, has a range of children and genealogy sites.

5. Online Historical Newspapers

Use your search engines. These sources often have free trials for a short period:

- British Newspaper Archive
- Canada Newspaper Archives
- Chronicling America
- Elephind
- Explore **news.google.com/newspapers**
- GenealogyBank
- Irish historical newspapers (at findmypast.ie)
- Papers Past
- trove.nla.gov.aus
- Wales newspapers

6. Family History Organisations
- Check **familyhistoryfederation.com** for England and Wales
- Check **www.safhs.org.uk** for Scotland societies
- Check **nifhs.org** for Northern Ireland
- Check **www.familyhistory.ie** and **www.ifhs.ie** for Ireland

7. Maps
Maps are often enjoyed by young family members and many are found online at no cost. There are many free sites such as: **maps.nls.uk**; **oldmapsonline.org**; **booth.lse.ac.uk** and **British-history.ac.uk/map.aspx**. These are samples, so use your search engines.

8. Electoral Rolls, Censuses and Directories
- United Kingdom electoral rolls and census returns are available on primary research sites, in 1 above, and free sites such as **freecen.org.uk**. The census years, every decade 1841–1921, are readily available on Ancestry, Findmypast and Scotland's People. However, in Ireland, see **www.census.nationalarchives.ie** for the 1901 and 1911 census returns. Only a few remnants of earlier censuses remain.
- Check on registers of trade and professional occupations. There are also locatable special collections, such as le.ac.uk which has trade directories going back to the 1700s. See church membership listings and the spinning wheel entitlement list or spinning wheel premium list.
- In Ireland, see Tithe Applotments, recorded, 1823–1837, listing workers on the land or who rented land. National Archives of Ireland site of these people is seen at **http://titheapplotmentbooks.nationalarchives.ie**
- In Ireland, see Griffith's Valuation which was carried out in the period, 1848–1864, recording landowners and dwellers in every parish in Ireland who were assessed for tax and the persons recorded by Griffiths can be found in specific online searches.
- Begin with Townlands, the smallest civil districts in Ireland. People were known by their townland. A historical 1837 topographic dictionary is available at: **www.libraryireland.com.topog/index.php**. Then locate parishes.

9. United Kingdom National Resources

Wales
- National Library at library.wales (wills, marriage bonds and parish records)
- Check localities and maps on places.library.wales and newspapers.library.wales

England
- National Archives England **www.nationalarchives.gov.uk**
- Society of Genealogists Library **www.sog.org.uk**

Scotland
- **www.nls.uk/digital-resources**
- **scottishindexes.com**
- ScotlandsPeople at **www.scotlandspeople.gov.uk**
- **www.nrscotland.gov.uk**

Northern Ireland
- Public Record Office Northern Ireland. Google PRONI and the site leads you into their informative world.
- Ulster Historical Foundation

Ireland
- The National Library of Ireland at **www.nli.ie** is helpful on genealogy. They have a guide at **www.nli.ie/en/family-history-introduction.aspx**
- The National Archives of Ireland is a free site
- Irish Genealogical Research Society **www.irishancestors.ie**
- Magazines: *Irish Lives Remembered*, *Irish Roots*, the *Irish Genealogist*
- Check out irishgenealogy.ie as the site of the General Register Office's births, marriages and deaths records plus others
- **www.irishfamilyhistorycentre.com** informs on webinars and podcasts
- Catholic sources **https://archive.catholic-heritage.net/default.aspx** catalogue is relevant for the United Kingdom and Europe archives
- Check Irish domains within Ancestry (especially Catholic), Findmypast and other primary sites
- Emerald Ancestors (emeraldancestors.com)
- RootsIreland (**www.rootsireland.ie**)
- Maintain the free online receipt of family history magazines' newsletters

10. Find a Grave and/or Tombstone

- BillionGraves
- Commonwealth War Graves Commission at **cwgc.org** for 2 million graves
- Deceased Online **www.deceasedonline.com** for United Kingdom
- FamilySearch has burial and cemetery records
- Find A Grave
- Findmypast has burial and cemetery records
- Historical newspaper death and obituary notices
- National Burial Index (England and Wales)
- War cemeteries

11. Military

- Search engines rapidly bring a range of sites. Try to obtain, from official military or government sources, the subject's service number, service alliance (regiment, ship or air force squadron) and, if available, their service record.
- See Fowler (2017). See White (1992).
- Many free online sources will help you. Check the linking site of **www. ukmfh.org.uk**.

12. Podcasts and Webinars

These can contain excellent information. Be aware – building up a lengthy list places demands upon time and tasks. Check them out. A good use of time is to divide the podcasts list with a family member or friend. Not only does this save time for each of you but valuable information gleaned from one of the pair's podcast listening can readily be shared with the other. You can use aids such as Spotify or iTunes for downloading a favourite podcast. Use a search engine to locate 'best genealogical podcasts' or 'family history podcasts' but also check podcast sites such as *Genealogy Gems, The Family Tree Magazine Podcast* and *Genealogy Gold* to sample good material. Webinars are available on a range of sites that search engines will locate. Family history magazines regularly mention them and their free access.

13. Photograph Enhancement

Family photographs are often a little blurred or lack the clarity we desire. There are many easily searched online sources of assistance for the keen researcher to develop clearer and soundly coloured pictures. A special children's favourite is the Deep Nostalgia programme on MyHeritage, guiding you to create smiling and moving images from still photos.

Photograph care makes **bl.uk/conservation/guides** a site to check and you can download a free guide. Enhancing photographs can readily be searched online or found in family history magazines. Examples follow:

- Adobe Photoshop
- JoyFlips
- MyHeritage
- Scantip.com
- Vivid-pix
- Vuescan

14. Searching Beyond the United Kingdom and Ireland

Australia & New Zealand
- For immigration to Australia, see **www.coraweb.comau/shipindex.htm** and check passenger lists on primary sites for ship lists to Australia, USA, Canada and New Zealand
- Archives New Zealand at **https://archives.govt.nz**
- National Archives Australia at **www.naa.gov.au**
- National Library, Australia at **www.nla.gov.au**
- National Library, New Zealand at **https://natlib.govt.nz**
- Papers Past for New Zealand historical newspapers
- See Hicks (2016) for Australia sources
- Trove for Australia historical newspapers

USA
This is search engine territory.

- The author's family has discovered One-Step Webpages, which is a well-organised site, solid in USA pointers for further research. If you are chasing an ancestor who may have moved to the USA, this site is worth an examination, as are Statue of Liberty-Ellis Island site, Castle Gardens and Access to Archival Database (AAD).
- The USA National Archives and Record Administration has archives.gov with a wide range of records.
- Immigration records at **http://search.ancestry.com/search/db.aspx?dbid=7486** is a must to start with.

Europe

Get search engines to do the work:

- Try The FamilySearch Research Wiki
- GeneaNet, a free site
- Remember you can find free online translations for material recorded in an unfamiliar language
- Family history magazines have excellent advisory articles on researching European records. Search the *Family Tree Magazine* for these, for example

Appendix II

AN OVERVIEW OF ONE FAMILY'S RESEARCH ADVENTURE

This appendix illustrates how one family's members, often with input from friends, sequentially developed their family history research with cross-generational participation. It includes the family's responses to certain results as examples of successes and tribulations. Some latitude has been self-permitted, drawing from friends' research to add to the reader's awareness of possible searches beyond the basic search sites. The phases are not rigidly determined but indicate broad progressive stages of the family's research.

Phase One

1. Beginning with fact gathering: information from family members
2. Obtaining BMD certificates or notices
3. Learning to utilise Ancestry, Findmypast, FamilySearch, MyHeritage
4. Searching historical newspapers

The author was too young to discuss family origins with his McConnell grandparents, but he was fortunate in discussing family history with his grandfather, Norman Charles Kensington. This grandfather's father had left a historic cursive handwritten history, in his 1890s surveyor's notebook, of the Kensingtons of Wiltshire and London. The direct tree was listed back to the 1480s. It led to those who married into the direct Kensington line. Certificates were obtained and, over some years later, they stimulated the searching of internet sites, particularly Ancestry, Findmypast and FamilySearch.

Extract re Amy Kensington (née Kenny) from her husband's surveyor notebook.

Then historical newspapers yielded information, including residential and occupational moves, appointments, ancestor migration, marriages and deaths. One of the deaths was the tragic death of the 1890s recorder's wife virtually outside his offices. The coroner decreed that the speed of the fire engine that struck Amy Kensington was excessive 'at twelve to fifteen miles an hour ...' (See Chapter 2, p.14.)

It was quickly noted, from interviews with older generation family members, and birth, marriage and death records, that the McConnells came from the Ballynagg district in County Antrim. Family legend told of their dispersal to Scotland, Canada and New Zealand. The family Bible gave a mix of birth, marriage and death information of three generations. The ancestor grocer's notebook told of the First World War recruit of a nephew of the grocer, found a world away. This led to a collateral ancestor.

Two partly detailed family trees were compiled of McConnell and Kensington direct lines.

Phase Two

1. Detailed searches were made, based upon Phase One records
2. Information from the wider family was sought
3. Electoral rolls were researched
4. Passenger lists and immigration records were checked
5. Search engines found further sites as research strengths
6. Persons who married into the direct ancestral line were traced

Collateral ancestors yielded more information, often through new links made by the researcher's family with first cousins, second, third and fourth cousins. We frequently turned to the major sources which we should have explored much more fully in the earlier phase. They became automatic sources to check whenever we found new leads from our wider research.

Electoral rolls, historical newspapers and archives gave us the William Henry Kenny family tree building up overseas but the Coleman family in County Louth and Johnston family in Longford was not so readily found, partly because of the common surname in Louth and partly because of an interchange of English and Irish first names. Searches of historical birth, marriage and death records from new lands led a trail from present to past and back again, often signposted with actual or potential information. Family timelines and historical timelines grew more detailed. Data from books and online sources led to questioning some of the 'facts' in the 1890s written family record.

Immigration and passenger lists became a focus as we tracked family and relatives. A nineteenth-century letter to United States, Australian and New Zealand newspapers from an Irish ancestor's family who were seeking contact with their migrated Coleman family member led to an examination of shipping lists for that person. Famine period shipping lists to various countries were located.

Family trees grew and brought new research challenges. A major focus now began in searches for those who had married into the direct line or had given birth with little information about them. This was sometimes challenging and still has some unresolved questions.

Phase Three

1. Record keeping and filing loomed larger than we expected
2. Family trees were continuously upgraded
3. Specialised sites were explored

4. PRONI and National Archives were visited
5. Ancestral locations in England, Wales and Ireland were visited

Record keeping and the organisation of files increasingly became important. The use of file boxes for separate families was a boon, but then we needed to become more familiar with setting up notes and files under ancestor surnames, then under sub-files of individual persons. Expert advice from a friend of a teenager led to Evernote and files being set up more efficiently on the computer. *Family Tree, Who Do You Think You Are?* and *Family Tree Magazine*, especially, were helpful in their articles on these. GEDCOM layouts were explored. Other suggestions were made to us of RootsMagic. We found helpful articles on filing and storage. These may not all have been followed, but they stimulated us to develop efficient storage modes.

Family trees were redrafted. After double-checking, we shared them with extended family members. This was appreciated by them and became a stimulus for them to search out material they had. Material from family members, not of the direct line, was becoming rewarding and led to more first-hand records about our direct ancestors, especially in the Maturin lines.

Living in Northern Ireland meant many days at the Public Record Office (PRONI) and some hours at Belfast Library and the Linen Hall library, researching McConnell, Stewart, McBride, Allison and Scott. (PRONI is essential for Northern Ireland and Ulster research.) Some handwritten church records from County Louth were difficult to read and this was compounded by our lack of Latin knowledge in religious terminology. We even turned to guidance from handwriting sites.

A step that had emotional overtones was learning about localities that figured strongly in the family. Census returns, historical newspapers, county archives, Google Earth, local histories, searches for maps and information from county genealogical and family history centres fostered our interest and knowledge. The **www.familyhistoryfederation.com/ societies-az** was searched and one locality offered a local family history person as our guide. (We found, much later, the Family & Community Historical Research Society, FACHRS.) Having facts established on places where family members lived, often for generations, led to a strong desire to visit those places. Again, that led to relatives, usually deemed to be 'distant relations', who proved to be as close as cousins.

Moving into specialised sites to follow up the accumulating factual material was rewarding and, as every genealogist experiences, often frustrating. We became more consistent in double-checking.

Puna McConnell outside Worton Church which was provided by Charles Snell Kensington.

Visiting ancestral homes and locations led to: photographs (such as Gayles and Worton); informative discussions with persons living in a past family home (as at Wernddu in Wales); burial sites (such as Colin Jones in Holyhead); cemeteries (as in Llanystumdwy) and family history interviews (such as in Dundalk). This generated a keenness to research an ancestor's home history, especially in Wales and Prince Hill in Worton.

Phase Four

1. Interludes of enjoyable exploration of family knowledge
2. Family stories assembled and shared
3. National Archives and National Libraries were explored
4. DNA testing was done
5. Family trees were double-checked and updated

We shared all information with siblings and this, at times, led to queries and suggestions. Certain family myths and stories, handed down over generations, added to the family's interest and knowledge of distant contemporary relatives. One close branch of the family shared an enjoyable range of home-made activities, puzzles and games over the years. Examples follow. These could be used at a family reunion.

1. True or False? Youngsters are provided with a list of ten ancestors, perhaps with their lifespans. A list is given of, say, fifteen historical happenings of which ten are to be placed with appropriate ancestors.

2. A simple crossword puzzle was constructed.

3. A world map was handed to each pair of contestants who had to place given ancestral names on relevant places.

4. The same challenge as in 3 (above) was done with a map of our country.

5. One part of the family later constructed a variation of what they called 'family monopoly' using family locations and old-fashioned crimes and punishments.

6. Variations of Trivial Pursuit and trivia challengers were easily formulated.

7. Jumbled names of ancestors were given out for sorting.

8. A set of fifty-two family picture playing cards was easily compiled for games which mirrored conventional card games or introduced new family history games. 'Patience' was popular with two children.

9. Artwork, writing, visual memorabilia, photographs and newspaper headlines were given out as two sets of playing cards. This led to a form of 'Snap' as youngsters had to recognise the relevance of their displayed card to the ancestor picture or ancestral fact turned up and displayed on the top of the pile of the other cards.

10. Photographs were displayed chronologically and the observer had to put the name of the person or place on their answer sheet. There were non-related people and even cartoon characters, displayed to further the enjoyment.

11. Home games played by ancestors were introduced. Tiddlywinks, from the times of 1880s forebears, was introduced to the author and his siblings when young. 'French Cricket', with its obscure origins, was played across generations. These generated youngsters' interest in the leisure pursuits of ancestors.

12. Family history word puzzle sheets were enjoyed. They included word lists of ancestors, places and ancestral facts with letters missing and each had to be completed e.g. Holyhe--, S-ory, Madra-, -ensington, Ma-urin, Chilc---. Jumbled names were a variant puzzle.

13. Marbles games from grandparents' childhoods were introduced. Some had been taught to the author and his siblings by their father. A new set of marble game idioms was learned.

14. Lists of first names and surnames were given, with linkages to be sorted.

15. Simple chronologies were to be placed in order. This led to one young researcher listing world events and challenging siblings, parents and grandparents to list contemporary ancestors for events.

16. Lists of ancestors and/or places were to be placed in alphabetical order.

17. Given ten family names, the family researchers had to write down one fact for each.
18. Games, quizzes. puzzles and activities would later be compiled on-screen, on USBs, phones and iPads and readily included documents, photographs, and factual information with illustrations.
19. 'Places and Persons' became popular, some years later, with grandchildren when a list of places had to be matched with a list of ancestors … with appropriately wrapped chocolate rewards!

A revised set of family trees was formed of each of the parents' ancestral lines. Checks of the trees were made with extended family members. At this stage, we needed to have consistent terminology for certain generations of ancestors, such as the clarification of cousins at different generational levels. This need for terminology accuracy became more accentuated when communicating between extended family members.

A family death in the First World War in Gallipoli.

We also rechecked print, diary and notebook sources we had from earlier generations. We found we had missed some helpful references to people and certain facts that led us to closer links between family and historical events. A grandfather's stained notebook had a note of a war death in the family which we had previously missed.

The National Archives (TNA) were visited at Kew, England. This is an inhibiting experience in some ways, given the immensity of the resources. We did not allow enough time although the tube rail access was good. In Dublin, we found the sites of homes and churches that featured in our direct line. Their National Library was engaging. The General Register Office needed more time than we planned, especially when we located army births, deaths and marriages in the rear of index books there! National archives, national libraries and national institutions were later revisited online.

Phase Five

1. Widening the field: military records, school records, wills
2. Family localities revisited
3. Visiting cemeteries, online and in actuality

Having what appeared to be core facts and having searched historical newspaper sources, and obtained certificates of births, marriages and deaths, we moved to school records, local histories, local family history societies, revisiting FamilySearch and our basic sites. From the eleven schools' responses to our enquiries, we established the starting and concluding enrolment dates of the four siblings and the addresses of our six successive homes.

With an illegitimate grandmother it was heartening for the author to find her mother later married a German fisherman and that led to school records, locating an informative local history book and making welcome contact with a descendant of one of the grandmother's half-sister's descendants.

The discovery that National Archives in England at **https://familytr. ee/people** holds PCC (Prerogative Court of Canterbury) wills, 1384–1858, was a green flag. The Prerogative Court of York wills were more challenging.

Frustration can come from being unlearned about context and regulations of a particular era or country. This came with a military ancestor's marriage which was located in Canada in 1840. A discovery of military chaplain returns confirmed a second marriage and death for a military ancestor in India. The searches of National Archives and National Libraries of the United Kingdom countries and Ireland were illuminating. FIBIS (Families in British India Society) was joined as was the Guild of One-Name Studies.

Having increased knowledge, and a consequent better use of time, family areas were revisited or visited anew. More time spent in Llanystumdwy led to finding invaluable books related to our Welsh ancestry. The '*Pedigrees of Anglesea and Carnarvonshire Families*' (Griffith, 1985) was an exciting discovery. (See bibliography.)

In Salisbury Cathedral we felt the marriage of our direct ancestors, John Kensington and Myhill Blackwell in 1602. (Later, January 2021 newspapers featured the cathedral as a sanctuary where people received the Covid-19 vaccine were understood by youngsters in our family.)

In Worton and Potterne, our Kensingtons and Spearings had lived. The author's son knew of this and was delighted to find the memorial in the

Worton Church to Charles Snell Kensington, who had donated land and material assistance for the church. An indefatigable third cousin family researcher, Louise Buckingham, located a series of letters to the church from Kensington. See *Travelling with the Kensingtons* (2010) by Louise Buckingham and Ann Buckingham. This is an exemplary example of a family history book.

Southwell and Farnsfield in Nottinghamshire, with strong Watson and Clay linkages, over generations, brought similar pleasures. Checking Southwell resources led to Parish Chest with one of its products being some 300 years of Southwell marriages. Diary entries from family locale visits were written up for descendants.

The autobiography *On Record* (Paul's Book Arcade, 1962) of Isaac Coates had been given to the author when he was researching Coates and Coleman ancestors. This eventuated in time again being spent in Gayles, North Yorkshire, his initial home, and fostered new meanings of family history.

Friends of friends took us to North Yorkshire from Consett, in Durham, on a memorable day. The area still has Fenwicks, Coates, Parlour, Bainbridge, and Shaw relations. It felt dislocating when we drove away.

With the visits providing new stimulation, the family trees were updated and, in some cases, corrected. However, dead ends were still encountered. An aggravating example was finding absolutely no information on Allice Granger, mother of William Henry Granger (William Henry Kenny) born in 1811 in Tasmania – in contrast to locating the wonderful online list of 'Clays in Nottinghamshire'.

Gayles Village near Kirkby Ravensworth, Yorkshire.

This led to a more systematic search of tombstones and funeral records. Photographs of cemetery headstones, places and records assumed importance.

Personal circumstances then overrode the family history when Puna was diagnosed with leukaemia. This led to substantial changes in our life and living family history underscored each day. The death of that peerless woman led to a range of family history material that has given real sustenance in the years since, especially the life support letters and memories written by young ones in the family. What became her inevitable journey led to a rich vein of today's family writing for tomorrow's family.

Phase Six

1. Memorabilia were organised more definitively.
2. Individuals of interest became the focus of later research.
3. Books with family history relevance were given to children and grandchildren for their children.
4. This phase offered options for family members to follow their particular interest.
5. Summaries of research were always shared between siblings in four countries. Now there are two.
6. Photographs were shared and enhanced.
7. A wider range of family DNA testing was done.
8. Systematic collections were compiled to be critically reviewed for the family time capsules.

Puna's death led to substantial writing of the inevitable journey and the amazing woman, herself. This phase is ongoing. Family tree searches began to bring rediscoveries of memorabilia. A time capsule box of family material was developed for each grandchild. Memorabilia were given to their parents. These include: the original miniatures of ancestors of the eighteenth century; special presents; watches; an engagement ring; signed letters to and from family members; the small mother-of-pearl tray from Aunt Bella to her sister c.1900; signed letters and autographed photographs from legendary sportsmen; the birthday card and inscribed biography to Puna from Joan Sutherland; books given to each other by my grandparents (Ethel Alberta Coates and Norman Kensington) with lovingly formal inscriptions; a graduation gown; my father's tools and other prized possessions. Unexpected work was done to record the history of each of these, to have the value of some assessed, decisions made on which were to be given to living family and which would become possessions through a will. We documented some memorabilia with insurance details and took photographs of all the materials to be placed safely with valuations and receipts. A daughter suggested their safe storage in the event of theft or misfortune.

The death of John, our youngest brother, living in Texas, led to a lengthy set of 'John Stories' about growing up, which went to all nephews and nieces. These have become richly anecdotal accounts when told with relish by grandchildren. My sister has become the outstanding genealogist in our family in a pleasing role-change.

The online search net spread. Youngsters now began to actively track down selected ancestors who took their interest. Interest in Gabriel Maturin heightened with the discovery that the man in the so-called Iron Mask was imprisoned at the same time and place. Finding first-hand material for this present book led to many rediscoveries. A 1981 birthday card from my son, then 8 years old, declared 'P.S. Colonel Kenny's watching you'! The Colonel had died in 1880! My daughter wrote imperishably of Puna. The family stories resonated in some mysterious ways. We are what we are becoming – not what we have become.

Research continued, albeit spasmodically at first. Certain ancestors stimulated research on their lives and time. Researching the author's direct Kensington line in Worton, Wiltshire, led to the discovery of a bachelor uncle who loomed as a prominent 'whole-family' figure. We discovered that Charles Snell Kensington had been imprisoned in France during the Napoleonic Wars, where he fell in love, and had a son who lived for but two years. As a non-combatant prisoner of war he had to give his 'Word of Honour' not to escape to England.

DNA tests were carried out by three siblings through Ancestry, MyHeritage and 23andMe. The family history then shifted on the axis of what had previously seemed to be a full account of McConnell ancestry. We found that our father's legal father was not his biological father. That caused a doubletake across the family. This became conclusive and a whole new family line of Story was taken up rather than McConnell. Literally, some half a century of McConnell ancestry research, from older generation interviews, to the family Bible, to letters and official certificates was now redundant.

Be warned that such things can arise for any person obtaining DNA results. This new path of ancestry, however, led to new Story cousins and family trees. It was uplifting to meet a cousin whose father and ours were biological half-brothers. This raised questions of how to pass such new knowledge on to our own children, cousins and wider family members. It was challenging yet exhilarating. This was a family history research adventure, classified initially for adults only! The new lineage confirmation led to a loved aunt's DNA which confirmed that she, also, was the biological daughter of Dr Story. This led to a closer examination of that generation in family photographs.

To add to this DNA revelation, another set of DNA results led to us being contacted by a deceased brother's natural daughter.

As the bulk of basic records had been relatively fully searched, to the present, the author's son and daughter persuaded him to start his personal life history, for them and their children. That is the goal for 2022. I realise now, more than ever, that family history will be as much about who they are as who their father is. Each of their children has an interest in their family history, being shaped in part, by identifying with their own narratives of becoming. We do not age into the past but into the future. For the family historian the search goes on. Then, we are suddenly confronted with a break in that direct line narrative when we encounter the strangely uplifting bleakness of a family tale that compels our full attention. This last family history discovery, in 2021, is one such story.

The Story that Draws Family and History Together

For each of us, our family history is alive and continuing. Its latest discovery, in 2021, is a rare and tragic example that graphically draws together the whole-family approach to research. In tracing a collateral ancestor, we drew more to a direct ancestor. Isaac Coates, of the Coates

Three generations with collaterals!

family North Yorkshire, migrated to New Zealand in 1862. Among distant relations of Coates were Bainbridges. Coates' great-grandson was informed, in 2021, of a distant link between Edwin Bainbridge of Northumberland and Isaac Coates. Coates' eldest descendants in New Zealand remember being told that Edwin was determined to visit New Zealand to see the markedly wonderful Pink and White Terraces, near Rotorua, then intended to visit his Coates relation, in Hamilton.

Edwin's life had been marked by tragedy. His father died when Edwin was 7 years old, and his mother died before he was 9 years old. Edwin's brother was killed in 1885 in a shooting accident and his sister died of consumption. Edwin, an enthusiastic amateur explorer, was 20 years old, seeking stability and desperately wanting to travel and be well distanced from his home area.

Arriving in Auckland in 1886, his fellow tourists decided to stay in the city, so Edwin journeyed down to Te Wairoa, alone, to see the Pink and White Terraces, a lifelong ambition. He was the only guest at the Rotomahana Hotel. He walked and explored and spent time with the legendary Guide Sophia, who told him of the foreboding ghost canoes she had recently seen. She noted unusually active thermal movements on the lake as they journeyed across. However, when Edwin stood before the world-renowned Terraces he felt his long journey was worthwhile.

That night of 10 June 1886 was shattered with eruption. Eventually, onlookers – in trepidation – moved to the hotel to join its sole occupant. Earthquakes shook the hotel and stones and ash hurtled onto the roof.

Edwin's diary states:

Written by Edwin Bainbridge of Newcastle on Tyne, England. This is the most awful moment of my life. I cannot tell when I may be called upon to meet my God. I am thankful that I find His strength sufficient for me. We are under heavy falls of volcanic …

The nervous group decided to evacuate the hotel and move to Guide Sophia's home. As they left the hotel, the veranda roof buckled under the weight of volcanic mud and stones and fell suddenly upon Edwin. He was the last person killed in the destructive eruptions that destroyed the Pink and White Terraces.

Some 150 kilometres (93 miles) away, Isaac Coates was expecting Edwin to arrive sometime in June, but did not know where his kinsman was. Coates' diary noted in 1886:

On the night of June 10th … a very great eruption took place in the Wairoa Valley near Rotorua … I could not sleep for the great noise and the big flashes of fire, high in the sky … I may mention that one English tourist lost his life at the Wairoa Hotel, a portion of the hotel falling upon him … The hotel was a wreck but perhaps the greatest loss was the Pink and White Terraces, all of which were destroyed, being completely blown up.

Coates did not know, at that time, the tourist was his kinsman, the 20-year-old Edwin Bainbridge. In a cemetery near Rotorua is an obelisk memorial, which Edwin Bainbridge's family in England have had erected.

There is hardly a more graphic or heartfelt family link between a family timeline and a historical timeline. The destruction of the Pink and White Terraces, sometimes noted as the eighth wonder of the world, is known by archaeologists worldwide. This Coates-Bainbridge account arose from various sources that realistically illustrate the family use of research.

Search engines seeking online Coates family trees had led to research on families that married into the family. This led to contact with a compiler of one tree, the fourth cousin from the Gayles-Kirkby Ravensworth area where Coates families lived. The fourth cousin noted the Coates-Bainbridge link. The author recalled a family story that a Bainbridge visited Isaac Coates in New Zealand. Passenger lists were searched. Historical newspaper accounts in New Zealand and England were searched.

Online searches led to the informative 'The Buried Village of Te Wairoa Blog' whose source supplied information significant in the account above, with their permission.

A graphic first-hand source was Edwin Bainbridge's diary, which was found under the rubble of the eruption. Isaac Coates' diary records are in his book *On Record*, the use of which had been granted to the author who is writing Coates' biography.

Children, young family members and adults contributed results of their online searches which validated the above account. The stark reality and faith of Edwin Bainbridge has resonated in our family with young and old for whom Isaac Coates is in their direct line and Edwin Bainbridge is now an inner companion in their walk through history. They now have a nigh-perfect example of history timelines and family timelines intersecting.

To Sons and Daughters of Coming Years

May you trail your fingers
in blue rivers of time,
run in meadows after rain, and
find love that stops you in your tracks
with the first glimpsed intensity
of a promised land
and may you embrace
a happy life of service
but have no less the service
to self than to others,
and may you know that self
and kindle your dreams,
roll in the greenest of grass,
take lessons of life as gifts
for your growing,
and have a heart that will
laugh often at the absurd
and weep a little for the needy.
Becoming stars on our leaving
we shall endeavour to light your path
as you step out in sometimes hesitant truth
and, then, when you
reach for the stars, we will
mark the way and our love will guide you.

BIBLIOGRAPHY

Beller, Susan Provost, *Roots for Kids,* (Genealogical Publishing Co., Baltimore, 1989).

Bennett, Sharon Combs, 'Can You Claim a Coat of Arms Based on Your Last Name?' (*Family Tree Magazine*, January–February 2018).

Blake, Paul & Loughran, Maggie, 'Irish Wills From 1858', (*Who Do You Think You Are Magazine*, Issue 173, January 2021, pp 61–5).

Blanchard, Gill, *Writing Your Family History* (Pen and Sword, Barnsley, Reprint, 2021)

Brasch, R., *How Did Sports Begin?* (Angus & Robertson, Sydney, 1995)

Buckingham, Louise & Buckingham, Ann, *Travelling with the Kensingtons,* (Ann Buckingham, Wellington, 2010).

Chorzempa, Rosemary A., *My Family Tree Workbook,* (Dover Publications, New York, 1982).

Christian, Peter, *The Genealogist's Internet,* (London, Bloomsbury, 2012).

Coates, Isaac, *On Record* (Paul's Book Arcade, Hamilton, New Zealand, 1962)

Cornwell, Bernard, *Sharpe's Fortress* (Harper Collins, 1998)

Crume, Rick, 'Gedcom: Opening and Sharing Files in 8 Steps', (*Family Tree Magazine*, Undated).

Emm, Adèle, *Tracing Your Female Ancestors* (Pen and Sword, Barnsley, 2019).

Fivush, R., Duke, M., & Bohanek, J., *'Do You Know…' The power of family history in adolescent identity and well-being.* (Marial Center, Emory University, Atlanta, 2010)

Fowler, Simon, *A Guide to Military History on the Internet* (Pen and Sword, Barnsley, 2009).

Fowler, Simon, *Tracing Your Army Ancestors* (Pen and Sword, Barnsley, 3rd Edition 2017).

Frazel, Midge, *Links to the Past Through Genealogy: Curriculum Activities for the Classroom* (Linworth Publishing, Worthington, 2005).

Frisch, Karen, *Creating Junior Genealogists* (Ancestry/Turner Publishing, New York, 2003).

Green, Benny, *Wisden Book of Obituaries* (Macdonald Queen Anne Press, London, 1986).

Greene, Bob & Fulford, D.G., *To Our Children's Children* (Doubleday, New York, 1993).

Griffith, John Edwards, *Pedigrees of Anglesea and Carnarvonshire Families*, (Wrexham, Limited Edition, Bridge Books, Wrexham, 1985, facsimile reprint of 1914 Edition).

Henderson, Warwick, *The Fascinating History of Toys & Games Around the World*, (New Holland Publishers, Auckland, 2018).

Hicks, Shauna, *Discover Your Sporting Ancestors*, (Gould Books, Ridgehaven, South Australia, 2015).

Hicks, Shauna, *Family History on the Cheap*, (Gould Books, Ridgehaven, South Australia, 2016).

Jones, J., *Gleanings from God's Acre*, (Richard Jones, Pwllheli, 1903)

Kreisel Shubert, B., *Out of Style: An Illustrated Guide to Vintage Fashions 19th–21st Centuries* (New York, 2nd edition. Dover, 2018).

Lima, Anna, *Family History and Genealogy: The Benefits for the Listener, the Storyteller and the Community* (Journal of Cape Verdean Studies. 4 [1] pp 63–74, 2019).

Lutz, Deborah, *The Brontë Cabinet. Three Lives in Nine Objects* (W.W. Norton, 2015)

McConnell, R.C., *Leadership and Extreme Sport* in *Berkshire Encyclopedia of Extreme Sports*, (Berkshire Publishing, Great Barrington, Mass., 2007).

McConnell, R.C., *Leadership: The Essential Key to Unlocking Family Team Potential*, (Faculty of Health, University of Canberra, 2011).

McConnell, R.C., *The Mysterious Tasmanian Origin of Colonel William Henry Kenny*, (Tasmanian Ancestry, Volume 41 Number 3 December 2020 pp 157–8).

Morton, Sunny Jane, 'Steps for Downloading a GEDCOM file from Ancestry.com' (*Family Tree Magazine*, noted online April 2021).

Niggemeyer, Vicki Korn, *Kids and Family History*, (Outskirtspress, Denver, 2017).

Oates, Jonathan, *Tracing Ancestors Through County Records* (Pen and Sword, Barnsley, 2016)

Paton, Chris, *Sharing Your Family History Online*, (Pen and Sword, Barnsley, 2021).

Paton, Chris, *Tracing Your Family History on the Internet*, (Pen and Sword, Barnsley, 2013).

Paton, Chris, *Tracing Your Irish Ancestors Through Land Records* (Pen and Sword, Barnsley, 2021).

Paton, Chris, *Tracing Your Irish Family History on the Internet*, (Pen and Sword, 2nd edition, Barnsley, 2019).

Paton, Chris, *Tracing Your Scottish Family History on the Internet*, (Pen and Sword, 2nd edition, Barnsley, 2020).

Resler, T.J., *Genealogy for Kids*, (National Geographic, Washington DC, 2018).

Rolling, Judy, 'The Power of Family History', (*Pediatric Nursing*. August 2013).

Rost J.C., *Leadership for the Twenty-first Century*, (Praeger, Westport Ct., 1991).

Scott, Jonathan, *The Family History Web Directory*, (Pen and Sword, Barnsley, 2015).

Shrimpton, Jayne, *Fashion and Family History*, (Pen and Sword, Barnsley, 2020).

Shrimpton, Jayne, *Tracing Your Ancestors Through Family Photographs*, (Pen and Sword, Barnsley, 2016).

Shrimpton, Jayne, 'Top 10 tips for studying the family photo album', (*Family Tree*, December 2020 pp 40–3).

Smith, Helen V., *Google the Genealogist's Friend*, (Gould Publishers, Ridgehaven, South Australia, 2016).

Wharncliffe Publishing/Family History Online, *Family History on the Internet*, (National Archives, Kew, 2010).

White, Arthur S., *A Bibliography of Regimental Histories of the British Army*, (The Naval and Military Press, Dallington, 1992).

INDEX